America's Deplorables

Timothy J. Amdahl

ISBN:1985132451
ISBN-13:9781985132450

DEDICATION

I dedicate this book to the millions of Americans whose voices are not regularly heard. To our great nation, and the millions that have gone before us and made this country what it is today. I give thanks to President Trump who willingly took on the duty as Commander-in-Chief. His life will never be the same. His private life now loomed with secret service, media, and strangers from afar. Thank you all who have contributed to making America great.

CONTENTS

ABOUT THIS BOOK

This book is about exploring the future of America. Our nation has been through rough times, some as we speak. While, we will cover many topics, know many of these, go back to the infamous swamps, Washington D.C.

As we go through these different topics, know I am going to offer my opinion, along with my philosophy. How will the left view me? As one American or as one of the Deplorable? To me I am proud to be identified as a deplorable, because we are making America one, while the Democrats focus on polluting our country with resistance, and no real direction of what needs to be done. They are out to disrupt, resist, and stall progress till their party can once again rein in the White House, giving them credit for all the accomplishments.

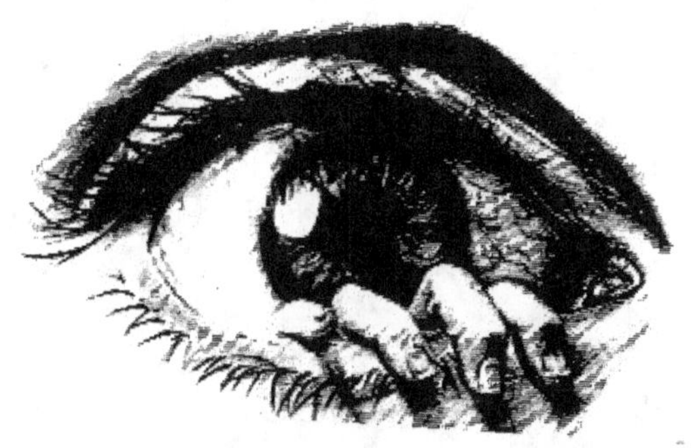

UNITED STATES
BIRTH OF OUR NATION

We will start off this book with immigration, as the United States of America was founded on July, 4th 1776. While this may be the day our country celebrates as our national holiday, the day we became an independent country, we must not forget our history, as we were not the first to arrive here.

Our country began with the settlement of Indigenous people, also called Indians, American Indians, Indigenous Americans. As of January 17th 2017 there were 567 Native American Tribes that were legally recognized by the Bureau of Indian Affairs. This agency is an agency of our federal government, made up by our people, or those that are employed through our government.

This agency fell underneath the Department of the Interior. This department was responsible for the administration and management of 55,700,000 acres of land held in trust by the United States, for Native Americans in the United States, Native American tribes, and Alaskan Natives.

The Bureau of Indian Affairs, is one of two bureaus that are under the jurisdiction of the Assistant Secretary for Indian Affairs. The other Bureau is the Bureau of Indian Education. This Bureau provides educational services to approximately 48,000 Native Americans.

If we go back before the United States, we see European settlers colonizing in the early 16th century. In the late 16th century, England, France, Spain, and the Netherlands launched major colonization programs in eastern North America. It took several decades to get established.

The European settlers came from many cultures and groups. These included adventures, soldiers, farmers, and tradesmen. They included the Dutch of New Netherland, the Swedes and Finns from New Sweden. There were the English Quakers from Pennsylvania. There were the Ulster Scots people, they were an ethnic group from Ireland. Their ancestors were mostly protestant lowland Scottish immigrants. The largest number of them coming from Galloway, Lanarkshire, Renfrewshire, Ayrshire, and the Scottish borders.

This is part of our history, it is here for us to remember, learn, and understand. To understand that our country was formed by a vast array of immigrants.

As we continue looking at immigration, we must also follow the birth of our country and understand the reason our country was formed in the first place. The thirteen colonies were a group of British colonies on the east coast of North America. They were founded in the seventeenth-and eighteenth centuries. In 1776 they declared their independence, forming the United States of America. The thirteen colonies had very similar political, constitutional, and legal systems and were dominated Protestant English speakers. They were part of Britain's possessions in the new world.

In the 18th century the British operated its colonies under a policy of mercantilism. This was a national economic policy designed to maximize the trade of a nation and historically, to maximize the accumulation of gold and silver.

As we move on to the Articles of Confederation, which was an agreement between the 13 original states of the United States of America. This served as its first constitution. It was approved after much debate, between July 1776 and November 1777.

The guiding principle of the Articles was to preserve the independence and sovereignty of the states. The federal government received only those powers which the colonies had recognized as belonging to king and parliament.

If we look at the next page, we will see the purpose for the Declaration of independence.

We hold these truths to be self-evident, that all men are created equal, that they are endowed by their Creator with certain unalienable Rights, that among these are Life, Liberty and the pursuit of Happiness. That to secure these rights, Governments are instituted among Men, deriving their just powers from the consent of the governed, That whenever any Form of Government becomes destructive of these ends, it is the Right of the People to alter or to abolish it, and to institute new Government, laying its foundation on such principles and organizing its powers in such form, as to them shall seem most likely to affect their Safety and Happiness.

Prudence, indeed, will dictate that Governments long established should not be changed for light and transient causes; and accordingly all experience hath shewn, that mankind are more disposed to suffer, while evils are sufferable, than to write themselves by abolishing the forms to which they are accustomed. But when a long train of abuses and usurpations, pursuing invariably the same Object evinces a design to reduce them under absolute Despotism, it is their right; it is their duty, to throw off such Government, and to provide new Guards for their future security.

All men are created equally

This clearly states, it is up to the people to see their government is put in check and that we the people keep them from putting us in harms. We must not forget our purpose for coming and creating the United States of America.

As we move from here to the constitution of the United States know it is the supreme law of the United States. Originally comprising seven articles describing the national framework of government. The first three articles establish the doctrine of separation of powers, whereby the government is divided in to three separate branches, those being Executive, which is overseen by the President, Legislative, run by the bicameral congress, and Judicial, consisting of the supreme court.

First Amendment, prohibits congress from making any law respecting an establishment of religion, impeding the free exercise of religion, abridging the freedom of speech, infringing on the freedom of the press, interfering with the right to peaceably assemble, or prohibiting the petitioning for a governmental redress of grievances.

Second Amendment, A well-regulated Militia, being necessary to the security of a free state, the right of the people to keep and bear Arms, shall not be infringed.

Third Amendment, No Soldier shall, in time of peace be quartered in any house, without the consent of the Owner, nor in time of war, but in a manner to be prescribed by law.

Fourth Amendment, The right of the people to be secure in their persons, houses, papers, and effects, against unreasonable searches and seizures, shall not be violated, and no Warrants shall issue, but upon probable cause, supported by Oath or affirmation, and particularly describing the place to be searched, and the persons or things to be seized.

Fifth Amendment, No person shall be held to answer for a capital, or otherwise infamous crime, unless on a presentment or indictment of a Grand Jury, except in cases arising in the land or naval forces, or in the Militia, when in actual service in time of War or public danger; nor shall any person be subject for the same offence to be twice put in jeopardy of life or limb, nor shall be compelled in any criminal case to be a witness against himself, nor be deprived of life, liberty, or property, without due process of law; nor shall private property be taken for public use, without just compensation.

The Bill of Rights, were written for our protection.

Sixth Amendment, In all criminal prosecutions, the accused shall enjoy the right to a speedy and public trial, by an impartial jury of the State and district wherein the crime shall have been committed; which district shall have been previously ascertained by law, and to be informed of the nature and cause of the accusation; and confronted by witnesses against him; to have compulsory process for obtaining witnesses in his favor, and to have the assistance of counsel for his defense.

Seventh Amendment, In Suits at common law, where the value in controversy shall exceed twenty dollars, the right of trial by jury shall be preserved, and no fact tried by a jury shall be otherwise re-examined in any Court of the United States, then according to the rules of the common law.

Eighth Amendment, Excessive bail shall not be required, nor excessive fines imposed, nor cruel and unusual punishments inflicted.

Ninth Amendment, The enumeration in the Constitution of certain rights shall not be construed to deny or disparage others retained by the people.

Tenth Amendment, The powers not delegated to the United States by the Constitution, nor prohibited by it to the States, are reserved to the States respectively, or to the people.

Eleventh Amendment, The Judicial power of the United States shall not be construed to extend to any suit in law or equity, commenced or prosecuted against one of the United States by Citizens of another State, or by Citizens or Subjects of any Foreign State.

Twelfth Amendment, The Electors shall meet in their respective states, and vote by ballot for President and Vice-President, one of whom, at least, shall not be an inhabitant of the same state with themselves; they shall name in their ballots the person voted for as President, and in distinct ballots the person voted for as Vice-President, and they shall make distinct lists of all persons voted for as President, and of all persons voted for as Vice-President, and of the number of votes for each, which lists they shall sign and certify, and transmit sealed to the seat of the government of the United States, directed to the President of the Senate. The President of the Senate shall, in the presence of the Senate and House of Representatives, open all the certificates and the votes shall then be counted.

The person having the greatest number of votes for President, shall be the President, if such number be a majority of the whole number of Electors appointed; and if no person have such majority, then from the persons having the highest numbers not exceeding three on the list of those voted for as President, the House of Representatives shall choose immediately, by ballot, the President. But in choosing the President, the votes shall be taken by states, the representation from each state having one vote; a quorum for this purpose shall consist of a member or members from two-thirds of the states, and a majority of all the states shall be necessary to a choice. [And if the House of Representatives shall not choose a President whenever the right of choice shall devolve upon them, before the fourth day of March next following, then the Vice-President shall act as President, as in the case of the death or other constitutional disability of the President.]* The person having the greatest number of votes as Vice-President, shall be the Vice-President, if such number be a majority of the whole number of Electors appointed, and if no person have a majority, then from the two highest numbers on the list, the Senate shall choose the Vice-President; a quorum for the purpose shall consist of two-thirds of the whole number of Senators, and a majority of the whole number shall be necessary to a choice.

But no person constitutionally ineligible to the office of President shall be eligible to that of Vice-President of the United States.

Thirteenth Amendment, **Section 1.** Neither slavery nor involuntary servitude, except as a punishment for crime whereof the party shall have been duly convicted, shall exist within the United States, or any place subject to their jurisdiction.

Section 2. Congress shall have power to enforce these article by appropriate legislation.

Fourteenth Amendment, **Section 1.** All persons born or naturalized in the United States and subject to the jurisdiction thereof, are citizens of the United States and of the State wherein they reside. No State shall make or enforce any law which shall abridge the privileges or immunities of citizens of the United States; nor shall any State deprive any person of life, liberty, or property, without due process of law; nor deny to any person within its jurisdiction the equal protection of the laws.

Section 2. Representatives shall be apportioned among the several States according to their respective numbers, counting the whole number of persons in each State, excluding Indians not taxed. But when the right to vote at any election for the choice of electors for President and Vice President of the United States, Representatives in Congress, the Executive and Judicial officers of a State, or the members of the Legislature thereof, is denied to any of the male inhabitants of such State, being twenty-one-year of age, and citizens of the United States, or in any way abridged, except for participation in rebellion, or other crime, the basis of representation therein shall be reduced in the proportion which the number of such male citizens shall bear to the whole number of male citizens twenty-one-year of age in such State.

Section 3. No person shall be a Senator or Representative in Congress, or elector of President and Vice President, or hold any office, civil or military, under the United States, or under any State, who, having previously taken an oath, as a member of Congress, or as an officer of the United States, or as a member of any State legislature, or as an executive or judicial officer of any State, to support the Constitution of the United States, shall have engaged in insurrection or rebellion against the same, or given aid or comfort to the enemies thereof. But Congress may by a vote of two-thirds of each House, remove such disability.

Section 4. The validity of the public debt of the United States, authorized by law, including debts incurred for payment of pensions and bounties for services in suppressing insurrection or rebellion, shall not be questioned. But neither the United States nor any State shall assume or pay any debt or obligation incurred in aid of insurrection or rebellion against the United States, or any claim for the loss or emancipation of any slave; but all such debts, obligations and claims shall be held illegal and void.

Section 5. The Congress shall have power to enforce, by appropriate legislation, the provisions of this article.

Fifteenth Amendment, Section 1. The right of citizens of the United States to vote shall not be denied or abridged by the United States or by any State on account of race, color, or previous condition of servitude.

Section 2. The Congress shall have power to enforce this article by appropriate legislation.

Sixteenth Amendment, The Congress shall have power to lay and collect taxes on incomes, from whatever source derived, without apportionment among the several States, and without regard to any census or enumeration.

Seventeenth Amendment, The Senate of the United States shall be composed of two senators from each State, elected by the people thereof, for six years; and each Senator shall have one vote. The electors in each State shall have the qualifications requisite for electors of the most numerous branch of the State legislature.

When vacancies happen in the representation of any State in the Senate, the executive authority of such State shall issue writs of election to fill such vacancies: *Provided*, That the legislature of any State may empower the executive thereof to make temporary appointments until the people fill the vacancies by election as the legislature may direct.

This amendment shall not be so construed as to affect the election or term of any Senator chosen before it becomes valid as part of the Constitution.

Eighteenth Amendment, Section 1. After one year from the ratification of this article, the manufacture, sale, or transportation of intoxicating liquors within, the importation thereof into, or the exportation thereof from the United States and all territory subject to the jurisdiction thereof for beverage purposes is hereby prohibited.

Section 2. The Congress and the several States shall have concurrent power to enforce this article by appropriate legislation.

Section 3. This article shall be inoperative unless it shall have been ratified as an amendment to the Constitution by the legislatures of the several States, as provided in the Constitution, within seven years from the date of the submission hereof to the States by the Congress.

Nineteenth Amendment, The right of citizens of the United States to vote shall not be denied or abridged by the United States or by any States on account of sex.

Congress shall have power to enforce this article by appropriate legislation.

Twentieth Amendment, Section 1. The terms of the President and Vice President shall end at noon the 20th day of January, and the terms of Senators and Representatives at noon on the third day of January, of the years in which such terms would have ended if this article had not been ratified; and the terms of their successors shall then begin.

Section 2. The Congress shall assemble at least once in every year, and such meeting shall begin at noon on the third day of January, unless they shall by law appoint a different day.

Section 3. If, at the time fixed for the beginning of the term of the President, the President-elect shall have died, the Vice President-elect shall become President. If a President shall not have been chosen before the time fixed for the beginning of his term, or if the President elect shall have failed to qualify, then the Vice President elect shall act as President until a President shall have qualified; and the Congress may by law provide for the case wherein neither a President elect nor a Vice President elect shall have qualified, declaring who shall then act as President, or the manner in which one who is to act shall be selected, and such person shall act accordingly until a President or Vice President shall have qualified.

Section 4. The Congress may by law provide for the case of the death of the persons from whom the House of Representatives may choose a President whenever the right of choice shall have devolved upon them, and for the case of the death of the persons from whom the Senate may choose a Vice President whenever the right of choice shall have devolved upon them.

Section 5. Section 1 and 2 shall take effect on the 15th day of October following the ratification of this article.

Section 6. This article shall be inoperative unless it shall have been ratified as an amendment to the Constitution by the legislatures of three-fourths of the several States within seven years from the date of its submission.

Twenty First Amendment, Section 1. The eighteenth article of an amendment to the Constitution of the United States is hereby repealed.

Section 2. The transportation or importation into any State, Territory, or possession of the United States for delivery or use therein of intoxicating liquors, in violation of the laws thereof, is hereby prohibited.

Section 3. The article shall be inoperative unless it shall have been ratified as an amendment to the Constitution by conventions in the several States, as provided in the Constitution, within seven years from the date of the submission hereof to the States by the Congress.

Twenty Second Amendment, Section 1. No person shall be elected to the Office of the President more than twice, and no person who has held the office of President, or acted as President, for more than two years of a term to which some other person was elected President shall be elected to the Office of the President more than once. But this Article shall not apply to any person holding the office of President when this Article was proposed by the Congress, and shall not prevent any person who may be holding the office of President, or acting as President, during the term within which this Article becomes operative from holding the office of President or acting as President during the remainder of such term.

Section 2. This article shall be inoperative unless it shall have been ratified as an amendment to the Constitution by the legislatures of three-fourths of the several States within seven years from the date of its submission to the States by the Congress.

Twenty Third Amendment, Section 1. The District constituting the seat of government of the United States shall appoint in such a manner as the Congress may direct:

A number of electors of President and Vice President equal to the whole number of Senators and Representatives in Congress to which the District would be entitled if it were a state, but in no event more than the least populous State; they shall be in addition to those appointed by the States, but they shall be considered, for the purposes of the election of President and Vice President, to be electors appointed by a State; and they shall meet in the District and perform such duties as provided by the twelfth article of amendment.

Section 2. The Congress shall have power to enforce this article by appropriate legislation.

Twenty Fourth Amendment, The right of citizens of the United States to vote in any primary or other election for President or Vice President, for electors for President or Vice President, or for Senator or Representative in Congress, shall not be denied or abridged by the United States or any State by reason of failure to pay any poll tax or other tax.

Section 2. The Congress shall have power to enforce this article by appropriate legislation.

Twenty Fifth Amendment, Section 1. In case of the removal of the President from office or of his death or resignation, the Vice President shall become President.

Section 2. Whenever there is a vacancy in the Office of the Vice President, the President shall nominate a Vice President who shall take office upon confirmation by a majority vote of both Houses of Congress.

Section 3. Whenever the President transmits to the President pro tempo re of the Senate and the Speaker of the House of Representatives his written declaration that he is unable to discharge the powers and duties of his office, and until he transmits to them a written declaration to the contrary, such powers and duties shall be discharged by the Vice President as Acting President.

Section 4. Whenever the Vice President and a majority of either the principal officers of the executive departments or of such other body as Congress may by law provide, transmit to the President pro tempo re of the Senate and the Speaker of the House of Representatives their written declaration that the President is unable to discharge the powers and duties of his office, the Vice President shall immediately assume the powers and duties of the office as Acting President.

Thereafter, when the President transmits to the President pro tempo re of the Senate and the Speaker of the House of Representatives his written declaration that no inability exists, he shall resume the powers and duties of his office unless the Vice President and a majority of either the principal officers of the executive department or of such other body as Congress may by law provide, transmit within four days to the President pro tempo re of the Senate and the Speaker of the House of Representatives their written declaration that the President is unable to discharge the powers and duties of his office.

Thereupon Congress shall decide the issue, assembling within forty eight hours for that purpose if not in session. If the Congress, within twenty-one-day after receipt of the latter written declaration, or, if Congress is not in session, within twenty-one-day after Congress is required to assemble, determines by two-thirds vote of both Houses that the President is unable to discharge the powers and duties of his office, the Vice President shall continue to discharge the same as Acting President; otherwise, the President shall resume the powers and duties of his office.

Twenty-Sixth Amendment, Section 1. The right of citizens of the United States, who are eighteen years of age or older, to vote shall not be denied or abridged by the United States or by any State on account of age.

Section 2. The Congress shall have power to enforce this article by appropriate legislation.

Twenty Seventh Amendment, No law, varying the compensation for the services of the Senators and Representatives, shall take effect, until an election of Representatives shall have intervened.

Under Article two of the Constitution of the United States, it strictly states, The Congress may determine the time of choosing the electors, and the day on which they shall give their votes; which day shall be the same throughout the United States.

No person except a natural-born citizen, or a citizen of the United States, at the time of the adoption of this Constitution, shall be eligible to the office of President; neither shall any person be eligible to that office who shall not have attained to the age of thirty-five years and been fourteen Years a resident within the United States.

I know this is a short view of the birth of our country, but it is the foundation and framework for which we are here today. Our country was founded on proud people that were willing to lay down their lives for the rest of us. They fought for a cause and for their independence. We have always stood for our people as well as our neighboring allies. This does not mean we have not struggled, we have.

We have always been seen as one of the superpowers, a country other's could reach out to for help. It is our morals and values, our spiritual beliefs that help guide us. We take pride in the way we salute, knowing we have never lost a war. We show our respect by standing for our flag and for our national anthem. We Americans put God first, then our country and us last. While this may not be true today, it was at the time our country was born.

As we continue on let us look at the history of the different parties that helped make our country what it is today. As we travel back in time, we will start with the Federalist party.

The Federalist Party, The Federalist Party was one of the first two political parties in the United States. It originated as an opposition to the Democratic-Republican Party during President George Washington's first administration. The Federalist Party remained a force till members had passed into the Democratic and Whig Parties in the 1820s. The party drew its early support from those who-for ideological and other reasons-wished to strengthen national instead of state power.

The Democratic-Republican Party, Democratic-Republican Party, originally (1792–98) Republican Party, first opposition political party in the United States. Organized in 1792 as the Republican Party, its members held power nationally between 1801 and 1825. It was the direct antecedent of the present Democratic Party.

The Whig Party, In 1834 political opponents of President Andrew Jackson organized a new party to contest Jacksonian Democrats nationally and in the states. Guided by their most prominent leader, Henry Clay, they called themselves Whigs, the name of the English antimonarchist party, the better to stigmatize the seventh president as 'King Andrew.' They were immediately derided by the Jacksonian Democrats as a party devoted to the interests of wealth and aristocracy, a charge they were never able to shake completely.

The Republican Party, Republican Party, byname Grand Old Party (GOP), in the United States, one of the two major political parties, the other being the Democratic Party. During the 19th century the Republican Party stood against the extension of slavery to the country's new territories and, ultimately, for slavery's complete abolition. During the 20th and 21st centuries the party came to be associated with laissez-faire capitalism, low taxes, and conservative social policies. The party acquired the acronym GOP, widely understood as "Grand Old Party,"

The Democratic Party, The Democratic Party has changed significantly during its more than two centuries of existence. During the 19th century the party supported or tolerated slavery, and it opposed civil rights reforms after the American Civil War in order to retain the support of Southern voters. By the mid-20th century it had undergone a dramatic ideological realignment and reinvented itself as a party supporting organized labor, the civil rights of minorities, and progressive reform.

The National Union, The National Union Party was the temporary name used by the Republican Party for the national ticket in the 1864 presidential election, held during the Civil War. For the most part, state Republican parties did not change their name. The temporary name was used to attract War Democrats and border states Unionists who would not vote for the Republican Party.

This first chapter was a brief overlay of the birth of our nation. It covers the constitution as it points out the rights the people have as well as defining we the people make up our government. It is us, who will keep our government in check.

We also look at the political side of our history as we look at the different political parties that have at one time governed our nation. Our history teaches us about our past, and to never forget. When our government was created, it was so that our government would never take over and become a dictatorship.

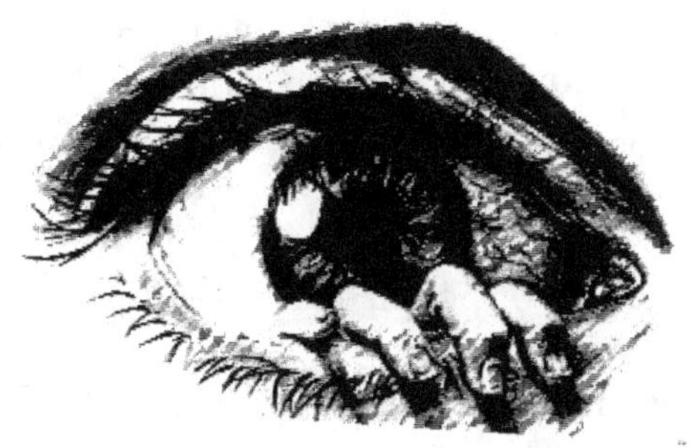

AMERICA'S BORDERS
BUILDING THE WALL

In this chapter we will cover our borders. The United States is a country that has always prided itself on being safe and out of harm's way. We saw to it that war was brought to the enemy and not here in our own land that we so dearly love and cherish.

On December 7, 1941, at 7:55 am. Hawaii time, the naval base Hawaii was attacked. We know this as Pearl Harbor. However, this was before Hawaii was part of the United States. Hawaii became a state on August 21, 1959. It was not officially a state at the time we were attacked. This affected Americans greatly. It was an attack on our U.S. Naval forces. As we continue, we bring up the infamous 9/11 attack that would forever change us.

On September 11, 2001, our country would stop in awe and utter disbelief, as we all witnessed what at the time seemed like a freak accident, when a plane later identified as American Airlines Flight 11 crashed into one of the Twin Towers in New York City. The news media was reporting live as we all paused trying to figure out how that could even happen. As we watched as they reported, suddenly out of nowhere came another plane. Just like the first one we all watched as United Airlines Flight 175 crashed into the other Twin Towers. We were all paralyzed with our eyes fixed on the crash and the thought of hundreds of people losing their lives.

I knew after the second plane crash, as did many others, that this was deliberate. The U.S. went and secured the skies as all flights were ordered to land, as they tried to identify and locate all planes that were unaccounted for. Minutes later as we're still watching we hear of American Airlines Flight 77 being hijacked and flown into the Pentagon. The plane crashed into the Pentagon like an arrow seeking its target, collapsing the western side of the Pentagon.
They announced that we are on code Orange, or Red. Another plane has been identified as missing, it was United Airlines Flight 93, which was hijacked and was being diverted to Washington D.C. The passengers on that flight, however fought back heroically as the plane was brought down by the passengers in a field near Shanksville, Pennsylvania. Those passengers saved many more lives while they gave their lives unwillingly.

We witnessed the two Twin Towers being brought down as they crumbled before us leaving a plume that will forever be engraved in our minds.

As we witnessed the scars on the Pentagon and discovered the down plane with more losses, we begin to hear of who the culprits were. They were nineteen Al-Qaeda terrorists.

Both 110 story Twin Towers were demolished, killing 2,752 people. Approximately 200 passengers were killed that were on American Airlines Flight 77. Flight 93 crashing caused another 40 fatalities. Building number seven, also was demolished within this violent attack.

On February 16,2002 nearly five months later, a murderous assault would go on, known as the Beltway Sniper attacks. Muslim snipers, Lee Boyd Malvo, and John Allen Muhammad, killed Kena Cook in Washington. These Muslim killers would continue killing another twenty-one more victims. Malvo believed Muhammad, who told him the ten million dollar ransom, would be used for building a utopian society for 140 Black children on a Canadian compound. This was according to one of the defense attorneys for Malvo. The following are the list of victims and events that unfolded.

Jay Ray Taylor, sixty years old was shot in Tucson, Arizona golf course, on March 18, 2002.

Paul J. Laruffa was killed in the parking lot of his restaurant in Clinton, Maryland, on September 5, 2002.

Rupinder "Benny" Oberoi was shot and wounded outside a liquor store in Silver Spring, Maryland, on September 14, 2002.

Muhammad Rashid was shot outside a liquor store in Brandywine, Maryland, on September 15, 2002.

On September 21, 2002 the Muslim snipers killed Million A. Woldemariam, 41 years old, in Atlanta Georgia, Claudine Lee Parker, 52 was killed in Montgomery, Alabama, Kellie Adams, 24 years old was shot in the neck. All three victims were outside a liquor store during the shooting.

On September 23, 2002, they kill Hong Im Ballenger, who was 45 years old outside of a beauty store in Baton Rouge Louisiana. On the same day, they kill James D. Martin, who was 55 years old, outside of a supermarket in Wheaton, Louisiana.

On October 3, 2002 James L. Sonny Buchanan, who was 39 years old, was shot as he mowed a lawn near a car dealership in White Flint, Maryland. Premkumar A. Walekar, who was 54 years old, was killed on the same day as he pumped gas at a station in Aspen Hill, Maryland. Sarah Ramos 34 years old, was another victim that day, as she was shot sitting outside a shopping center in Silver Spring, Maryland. Two more victims that day would be added to their death list, a 25-year-old Lori Louis Rivera, who was vacuuming her car at a Shell gas station, in Kensington, Maryland and 72-year-old Pascal Charlot who just was trying to cross at a corner in northwest Washington.

On October 4, 2002 the same snipers shot and wounded Caroline Seawell 43, as she was loading her car in Fredericksburg, Virginia.

Three days later, on October 7, 2002, Iran Brown was shot and injured. He was only 13 years old. He was shot outside the Nejamin Tasker Middle School in Bowie, Maryland.

On October 9, 2002 the snipers kill a Vietnam Veteran, Dean H. Myers, who was 53 years old, as he pumped gas in Manassas, Virginia. As we continue on here these two terrorist killed a 53-year-old Kenneth H. Bridges as he pumped gas near Massaponax, Virginia. Linda Franklin 47, was killed outside in a Home Depot parking lot in Falls Church, Virginia. Jeffery Hoppers was wounded as he walked his wife in a restaurant parking lot, in Ashland, Virginia. Conrad E. Johnson was killed standing in the doorway of his bus In Aspen Hill, Maryland on October 22,2002.

These two killers created a storm of fear, as they enjoyed taking lives of old, young, veterans, male, female, or anyone that they deemed were convenient for their pleasure. Many lives were affected by these killers.

I could have summarized this shorter, but then we lose the value of each one of these people's story. Each one was doing what they wanted to do in their own community, never harming no one. What did these people do wrong? Did they deserve this consequence?

These two people destroyed countless lives, due to their ideologies. John Allen Muhammad was a native of Jamaica West Indies.

The Spanish transplanted African slaves to Jamaica as laborers. Jamaica became a leading sugar exporter, with its plantation economy highly dependent on slaves forcibly transported from Africa. In 1838 the British emancipated all slaves.

On August 6, 2003 Mohammed Ali Alayed 23 years old, also the son of a Saudi Millionaire, slashes the throat of Ariel Sellouk, an estranged Jewish friend, killing and nearly decapitating him. The two had gone their separate ways close to a year when Mohammed Ali Alayed would show back up now more committed to Islam. He was identified as a religiously strict Muslim.

On December 2, 2003 a Jewish man, by the name Joseph Applebaum, suffers from the swelling of his stomach which should be easily diagnosed and treated, was refused treatment and left to die by a Muslim doctor.

April 15,2004, Ismail Pettek fearing that his brother had molested his wife and daughter, killed his wife by bludgeoning her on the head with a hammer, and attacked both his 22-year-old and 4-year-old daughters. He stated that he feared his family's honor had been taken. When asked if he would do it again and kill them he stated "My female family yes, my male family no."

In January 2005 a Somali immigrant, Mustafa Muhammed, 30 years old slashes and injures six people in a retirement home. In Alexandria, Virginia. One received 200 stitches while another received a broken neck. The judge found him not guilty by reason of insanity.

On March 3, 2006, Mohammed Reza Taheri-azar, an Iranian American, sought to avenge the deaths of Muslims worldwide, while punishing the United States government. He intentionally runs down injuring nine people at a campus in North Carolina.

On June 16, 2006, a 62-year-old Paul Schrum who is a Jewish man, was shot and killed as he was headed to the movies by 23-year-old Mujtaba Rabbani Jabbar, who happened to be Muslim. This happened in a heavily Jewish area in Baltimore, Maryland. Mujtaba shot him three times, then walked into the lobby setting the gun down on the counter as he waited for police.

On June 25, 2006, Michael Julius Ford 23, uses a long barrel handgun to shoot four Co-workers and a police officer in Denver Colorado. He had converted to Islam and claimed the attack was Allah's choice.

On July 28, 2006, Naveed Afzal Haq, identified as a Muslim man, shoots six women. One of the women died. He then grabbed a 14-year-old girl, using her as a hostage during the attacks. The officials classified the attack as a hate crime rather than as terrorism.

January 1, 2008, Yaser Said, an Egyptian-born cab driver, shoots and kills his two daughters in Irvin, Texas. He killed them because they were dating none Muslim boys. The daughters had run away from home a week earlier, fearing their father would kill them.

Two girls with nowhere to run

July 6, 2008, A 56-year-old Muslim Pakistani man by the name, Chaudry Rashid, strangles his 25-year-old daughter in Jonesboro, Georgia. She wanted out of an arranged marriage.

On February 12, 2009, Pakistani American Muzzammil Syed Hassan, who was a CEO of the first American Muslim TV network broadcast in English Bridge TV. Hassan beheaded his estranged wife, Aasiya Zubair after she had filed to divorce him. When he was arrested, he stated he felt an incredible amount of relief after killing the women.

April 12, 2009, a Muslim man shoots and kills his brother-in-law and another man in Phoenix, Arizona after he had found out that they patronized a strip club.

On June 1, 2009 Abdulhakim Mujahid Muhammad, a convert of Islam had traveled to Yemen was deported to the United States for over staying his Visa. He opened fired on some soldiers outside of a recruiting station in Little Rock Arkansas. Muhammad killed one private and injured another. He stated he was going to kill as many soldiers as he could and was given the assignment by Al-Qaeda in the Arab peninsula.

November 2009, a 48-year-old Faleh Hassan Almaleki, Iraqi born Muslim kills his daughter using a vehicle. Because she had become too westernized. He also attacked the boyfriend's mother. This all occurred do to his daughter not following traditional family values.

On November 5, 2009, a Muslim gunman who happened to be an Army Psychiatrist and was known as Nidal Milik Hassan, fatally shoots 13 people and wounds 30 others at Fort Hood Texas.

December 4, 2009, A Muslim graduate student from Saudi Arabia Abdulsalam S. Al-Zahrani stabbed his professor to death who was none Muslim. This was done to avenge the persecuted Muslims.

On April 14, 2010, A Muslim man, James A. Larry 33 years old, became angry that his family would not convert to Islam. He shot his mother, pregnant wife, and infant son, and two nieces In Marquette Park, Illinois. He also shot his 13-year-old nephew in the face, but he survived. He stated he wishes he had more bullets.

April 30, 2011, Rahim Abdul Alfetlawi 46, shot his stepdaughter in the head at point blank range, in Warren Michigan. She refused to adhere to Muslim customs.

On September 11, 2011, three Jewish men were found dead with their throats cut in Waltham Massachusetts. According to reports, the Authorities believe it was the work of Tamerlan Tsarnaev and his brother, both were associated with the Boston Marathon Bombing. Thousands of dollars and Marijuana were left at the scene untouched.

On January 15, 2012, Ali Mahwood-Awad Irsan, a 57-year-old Jordanian Muslim, gunned down medical student Gelareh Bagherzedah. He was a friend of his daughters. He was a Christian and denounced Islam.

He later kills his Christian Son-in-Law after his daughter married him without permission. Ali Mahwood-Awad Irsan was reported to had said, "I killed that bitch and your next, No one insults my honor as a Muslim and gets away with it."

February 7, 2013, a 28-year-old Yusuf Ibrahim shot two Coptic Christians to death and beheaded them in Buena Vista, New Jersey. He then removed their hands before burying them in an abandoned back yard.

March 31, 2013, Reshad Riddle, walked into a church in Ashtabula, Ohio shooting and killing his father, then raised his gun shouting, "that the slaughter was the will of Allah, this was the will of God."

April 15, 2013, two Muslim Chechen brothers Dzhokhar Tsamaev, and Tamerlan Tsamaev, detonate two pressure cooker bombs during the Boston Marathon, killing 3 people and injuring approximately 264 other people. Tamerlan was shot and then run over by his own brother. Dzhokhar had temporarily escaped, but was later captured in a boat in someone's backyard.

On August 4, 2013 34-year-old Daymond Agnew went to an Ace Hardware store with a purpose from Allah to help people, before he fatally stabbed 17 times, Daniel Joseph Stone, who was an employee.

On March 6, 2014 Registered sex offender James Crosby, 46, is accused of bludgeoning his lesbian daughter to death and shooting her lover in Port Bolivar, Texas. Police believe he then dumped the bodies near a ferry gate.

April 27, 2014—A 30-year-old Muslim man, Ali Muhammad Brown, is accused of shooting to death two men in Seattle and a man in New Jersey. According to local reports, he told police the killings were "vengeance" for U.S. actions in the Mideast. According to court documents, he said they were "just kills" and that he was "just doing my small part" as a self-styled Jihadist.

Sept. 25, 2014—Alton Nolen is accused of beheading a woman in Moore, Oklahoma. Co-workers reported that Nolen had been trying to convert them to Islam. Nolen reportedly used "some Arabic terms" during his attack and had an interest in beheadings. Nolen told a judge, "I'm Muslim. My question is, do you have any Muslims that can represent me as a Muslim?"

May 3, 2015—In Garland, Texas, Pamela Geller, along with her group the American Freedom Defense Initiative, hosted a "Draw Muhammad" event. Elton Simpson and Nadir Soofi of Phoenix responded to a call to "avenge the prophet" and traveled to Garland, where they were shot and killed by a security guard after he open fired in an apparent attempt to get into the building. The guard was wounded in the attack. Islamic radicals have since called for Geller's head, and vow to kill anyone who "blasphemes" Muhammad.

July 16, 2015—Four U.S. Marines were shot dead in an attack, reportedly by a lone Islamic gunman, on U.S. Navy facilities in Chattanooga, Tennessee. Two law enforcement sources told CBS News that the shooting suspect was identified as Muhammad Youssef Abdulazeez, 24.

Abdulazeez was born in Kuwait and emigrated to the U.S. where he reportedly became a naturalized U.S. citizen.

This is one reason we need to build the wall. Too many innocent Americans have fallen victim to these radical Islamic terrorists. We should be able to feel safe pumping gas, or sitting on a chair outside in our own community. We shouldn't have to look both ways before we cross the street for anything other than an approaching vehicle. How many lives could have been saved?

• What good is it if you own land if you can't protect it? Wouldn't you want a wall for protection, shielding you from the elements of terror?. Why are the Democrats and a few of the Republican politicians afraid to put up a wall and teach those from other countries the proper way to enter our country, our home? How many of these Democratic and few Republicans would sit back and do nothing as someone tried entering their homes illegally?

Our constitution is sacred to us Americans. The Muslim culture, with their sharia law is not a part of our western culture, or our American heritage. Is this group looking to infiltrate our country in order to contaminate it? Are they slowly building communities within our borders as they promote havoc on our society?

We have just covered the threat of violence that is being brought in to our country with poor border management, but what about the threat of our own economic structure? What do our borders say on this?

On the following website,
https://www.newsmax.com/Newsfront/Illegal-Immigrants-Welfare-American/2016/05/09/id/727875/
    The households of illegal immigrants receive an average of about $1,000 more annually in federal welfare benefits than do the households of non-immigrant recipients, a new analysis finds.

    According to the immigration control advocacy group, **Center for Immigration Studies**, which breaks down federal cost data from 2012, the welfare payout to likely illegal immigrant households averages $5,692 yearly, compared with the average $4,431 welfare payout to non-immigrant households collecting the benefit.

    The CIS analysis study points out illegal immigrants are barred from directly receiving welfare, but may obtain it through their U.S.born children. This is their loop hole, they just have children and process their paperwork through them. This is criminals knowing the system, along with taking advantage of state and Federal programs.

    All immigrant-headed households, legal and illegal receive an average of $6,241 in welfare, 41 percent more than the $4,431 received by a non-immigrant household on welfare, according to the analysis. If we look at the Center for Immigration Studies, their data is separated between the legal and illegal immigrants using Census Bureau data. This analysis shows that legal immigrant households make extensive use of most welfare programs while illegal immigrant households primarily benefit from food programs and Medicaid through their U.S. born children.

Low levels of education not a legal status is the main reason immigrant welfare use is high. An estimated 49 percent of households headed by legal immigrants used one or more welfare programs in 2012, compared to 30 percent of households headed by natives.

Households headed by legal immigrants have higher use rates than native households overall and for cash programs (14 percent vs. 10 percent), food programs (36 percent vs. 22 percent), and Medicaid (39 percent vs. 23 percent). Use of housing programs is similar.

Legal immigrant households account for three-quarters of all immigrant households accessing one or more welfare programs.

Less-educated legal immigrants make extensive use of every type of welfare program, including cash, food, Medicaid, and housing.

The overwhelming majority of illegal immigrants have modest levels of education; therefore, the high use of welfare associated with less-educated legal immigrants indicates that legalization would likely increase welfare costs, particularly for cash and housing programs.

These cover programs like (SSI) Supplemental Security Income, (TANF) Temporary Assistance to Needy Families, (WIC) Women, Infants, and Children food programs and (SNAP) Supplemental, Nutrition Assistance Program.

How much money is funded to assist those here illegally? In California, which is home to the largest number of illegal immigrants, they spent an estimated 1.2 billion dollars in 2017 through Medicaid to service 822,500 illegal immigrants.

The Federation for American Immigration Reform (FAIR). This group is a conservative advocacy group that favor tighter immigration laws. They state that illegal immigrants are costing us more than 100 billion dollars each year.

Let us look at how that affects the legal citizens of the United States. If we look at the homeless, we will see according to Social Solutions.Com, that 564,708 people are homeless in the United States. This consists of people living in the streets, cars, at shelters, or in subsidized transitional housing.

Here we see that we have a surplus of money to take care of illegal immigrants while we choose to turn our backs on our own. Out of those numbers, 206,286 were family members. One quarter of them were children. Is this not sad?

Why are we not using that 100 billion dollars to help fund the wall? Why refuse to pay for a wall that saves you money down the road?

You could give each homeless person a million dollars and set it up in a fund where it would be budgeted out to them monthly. Think about the interest it would draw. That's money back into the community.

Think of the streets littered with homeless being cleaned up and no one starving. While I don't condone free handouts to those that think everything should be handed to them. I do believe we as a nation, a community, should at least be willing to look at these people and try to help them.

We have illegal immigrants that are in our country for various reasons. Some reasons may be honorable while others are criminal. Since they are all here illegally, they are all criminals. Many have filled out the proper forms and are waiting patiently. We are basically telling them the only way we will let you in, is if you come here illegally. If we do not enforce our own rules and laws, then it is like not having any.

We can look back at Washington D.C. and see one of the reasons our immigration is set up this way, is because of political agendas.

President Obama, Hillary Clinton, along with a long list of other Democratic and some Republicans feed their agenda through votes by those that they feel they can sway, that being the Hispanic voters. The poor, the uneducated.

On the other side you have those that are proud Americans who hold strongly to their constitutional rights, hard workers, military families, gun owners, and religious Christians. Each group lobbing for their own cause.

Let no lobbyist organization influence our country with intensions of harm for its own selfish agenda.

President Obama supposedly received 71 percent of the Hispanic votes when he ran and won in his election. He received many African American votes as well. I see nothing wrong with legal votes because those votes are legal. Let me give you an example that will bring this out in the light better.

Senator Chuck Schumer talked about immigration reform as there was a six person Bi Partisan committee that announced a draft reform plan that could bring more than eleven million undocumented immigrants out of the shadows. This tells me those shadows are already here in hiding.

This is eleven million illegals that are not paying taxes. These Immigrants are not contributing to our financial goals of making America great.

Senator John McCain (R-AZ) said, Illegal immigrants "will have to pay back taxes and pay for their citizenship, so I do not see a scenario where it would cost us money," This is the art of manipulation and fancy lawyer wording. Where will they get the money to pay their back taxes and become legalized citizens? They will use money that is funded to legal immigrants. Why have they not yet paid their taxes?

We must not forget whose country this is. We should give homage to those that came before us, and those that have given their lives fighting for our country, that we have so graciously been allowed to have been raised in. We should not forget our history, for what is forgotten will only be repeated.

If you are one that feels flying the American flag during Cinco De Mayo offends you then you are one that puts yourself ahead of your country. If you are one that feels taking a knee during our National Anthem helps your cause be heard, then you are ignorant to the freedom our flag provides and to the meaning of the National Anthem.

If you are one that thinks your country owes you for you being born, then move to another country and watch as you witness all your rights disappear outside our borders as you look back in.

There are two sides to every story. The inside of the United States and the Outside. Either you want to live with law-abiding citizens that have come here properly and legally, or you wish to live with strangers and criminals who are willing to harm others.

United we stand divided we fall.

Liberals think everybody wishing to enter our country are good. We have already given names of people that were not looking out after our country's best interests, but theirs.

Some point, Liberals will have to open their eyes. and see our country has rights. We have the right to live safely and should not have to worry about whether our neighbors are radical terrorist or not.

The sign above shouts peace through hope and trust, unfortunately our enemy can never be trusted. We build peace through power. Bullies don't pick on other bullies, they pick on the weak, the passive, and the forgiving. The Liberals seem to forget that while they preach kindness; it is them that have become the aggressors. They are the ones that name call, threaten, and assault with defamation of character.

We need them to remember to practice what they preach.

Building the Wall

Securing the borders with a wall. President Donald Trump ran his campaign on this and he is following through. There are walls that are being designed and tested as we speak.

Areas where the wall is needed but may not be feasible will have security of another kind. Finally America's doors are being locked to once again create a safe place to raise our families.

While we Americans desire peace through secure borders, others desire borders that are weak for the purpose of criminal activity.

To those, of the criminal world. Know America is back better than ever.

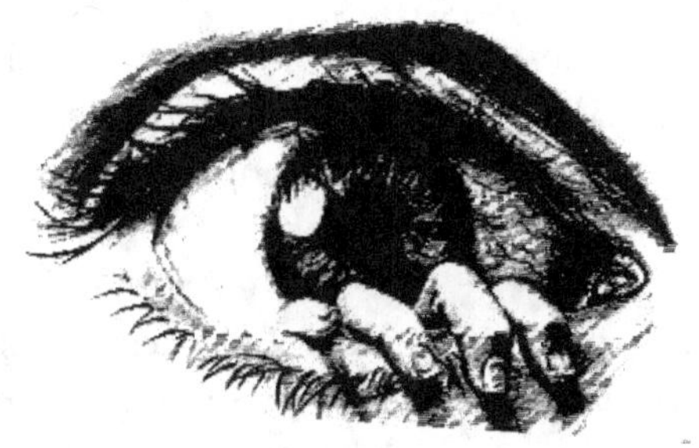

REIGNITING RACISM
Reverse Discrimination

Racism has been part of our culture a long time. Is it something I am proud of, No. Is it something we can overcome? Yes.

In this chapter we will try to understand what racism is, and from where it stems. As we look at our history know that it is you and I that determine our future. It is in our hands, how our fate will unite us, or divide us. Martin Luther King said he had a dream. Why can't his dream still live within all of us?

I too, have a dream. A dream where racism is no more. Where racism will be a part of our history only.

The definition of racism is. According to the *American Heritage College Dictionary*, racism has two meanings. Firstly, racism is, "The belief that race accounts for differences in human character or ability and that a particular race is superior to others." Secondly, racism is, "Discrimination or prejudice based on race."

I think that is a pretty accurate description. So where do we go from here? If we look at human behavior, we know that behavior can be genetic, cultural, or taught. The second part of racism is being a prejudice, or discriminating on a basis of race.

Is it racist to say an African American looks different, that they speak different, Are these racist opinions, or racist facts? If it is a fact, how can it be racist? It then becomes just a difference. I am just trying to get you to look at the difference between racism and being different. While we keep an open mind know that those that are racist are not opened minded, but rather close minded. They have already formed an opinion and seek to justify their opinion verse understand it.

While we will primarily be talking about racism between the African American culture, and the White Caucasian, know that it applies to all ethnic groups. As we step back in time, let's view another part of racism. The part where slavery was attached to a particular race. It is important to understand that some people of a particular race still feel very strongly that they are where they are today because of our past. We must first respect their opinion as history has left ugly scars. Remember scars heal all the time.

Let us travel back in time. Where did the first slaves come from? At the beginning of the 1600s, slaves for the Trans-Atlantic slave trade were sourced in Senegambia and the Windward Coast. The expansion of European empires pushed slavery as a cheap means of labor, along with lacking a strong workforce.

In 1619 at Jamestown in Virginia, there were approximately 20 Africans that were sold into slavery in the British North American colonies. In 1636 the Colonial North American Trade begins when the first American slave carrier named Desire is built and launched in Massachusetts. In 1641 Massachusetts is the first state to legalize slavery.

In 1662 Virginia enacts a law of hereditary slavery, which meant the child born of an enslaved mother inherits her slave status. This is sad, they were just seen as property. They could be bought and sold, never knowing when or where their future would take them. This was 355 years ago.

In 1676, 100 years before our country would fight for her independence, Black slaves and Black and White indentured servants would unite together and participate in what had become known as the Bacons Rebellion. It was the first rebellion in the American colonies. It was basically a battle between the ruling class and the Slaves, along with the poor.

Our history has been written, but not forgotten

In 1680, the state of Virginia did not allow Blacks and slaves to bear arms, or to gather in large crowds.

In 1682, Virginia declares that all imported Black servants are slaves for life.

In 1684 New York makes it illegal for slaves to sell goods. This you know was done for one reason, to make them dependent on their masters, owners, whatever you wish to title them as.

In 1691 Virginia passes a law forbidding Whites to marry Blacks, or Native Americans. South Carolina passes the first comprehensive slave codes.

In 1700 Pennsylvania legalizes slavery. Two years later New York passes an act regulating slaves on meetings of three or more slaves, trading by slaves, as well as a testimony of slaves in court. These stipulations were created to prevent Blacks from organizing. This kept them bound and helpless.

To add to this, in 1703 Massachusetts required every master who liberated a slave to pay a bond of 50 pounds or more. This was in case a freedman became a public charge.

As we move on to 1776 the year of our independence, it is at this time, that the Quakers in Pennsylvania forbid their members from holding slaves, along with the State of Delaware prohibits importation of slaves.

As we move on to 1777, we see that Vermont is the first of thirteen colonies to abolish slavery.

In this same year they also gave all adult males the right to vote. In New York they gave the right to vote to all free propertied men, regardless of color and their prior servitude.

In 1778 Rhode Island forbid the removal from slaves from the State. The State of Virginia prohibits importation of slaves as well.

In 1780, two years later Delaware makes it illegal to enslave imported Africans. The State of Pennsylvania begins emancipation gradually.

In 1783 Virginia emancipates those slaves that served in the colonial forces against Britain, provided their masters give permission. As we cover the next three years, we see that Rhode Island, Connecticut, North Carolina, and New York begin emancipation as well.

In 1785 Virginia deems any person with black blood to be a Mulatto and terms the use of the word Negro to be understood to include them.

In 1787 Richard Allen, a Black preacher, becomes the founder of the African Methodist Episcopal Church in Philadelphia, Pennsylvania. South Carolina ends domestic and international slave trade.

As we continue here, know these are the facts that are written in our history. While this all seems ugly, torturous, and uncivilized, it is a part of who we once were. Now, not everyone was for slavery. Many people opposed slavery.

What caught my attention as I was studying all this was how I viewed the Democrats as sympathetic to the African Americans. The truth is it was the Democrats that wanted slavery. It was the Republicans that fought to abolish slavery.

There is a lot more history out there that will show a continued battle for equal rights. We are now going to move closer to the present, about a hundred years closer.

In 1874 The Democrats win control of both Houses of Congress for the first time since the Antebellum years. The Whites regain control of the South Carolina Legislature.

In 1875 a Republican Congress passes a Civil Rights Act granting African Americans equal access to public accommodations, including transportation.

In 1902 Harry (Bucky) Lew was the first African American to breach the color line in professional basketball.

In 1918 African American troops fought in segregated units in World War I. The 360th regiment served longer in combat than any other unit. The Germans called them the Hell Fighters. The National Association for Colored People, (NAACP) formed a chapter by Harold M. Wingood.

In, 1920 the Ku KLUX Klan resurfaced after lying dormant. With over two million supporters. The 19th Amendment gave women the right to vote.

In 1937 Joe Lewis won the world heavyweight boxing title. As we move closer yet, in 1951 racial segregation in Washington D.C. restaurants is declared unconstitutional. During this time period, approximately 3500 Whites try to keep Blacks from moving in to Cicero. Hard to believe this was 67 years ago.

In 1952 The Tuskegee Institute reports that there
Hasn't been no reported lynching's in over 70 years. This is hard to visualize. Back in those days it was normal.. Racism will only change when we understand, it is a part of our history. There are more than one solution with solving this problem.

Let us remember that our country has struggled as well. We had the Civil War that put countryman against countryman. Families were divided on the battlefield. The Civil War is over. Most people have moved on. It is still a part of our history. There is nothing wrong with those people today still having pride in their heritage.

I look at it like I look back at graduating high school. I am proud I got a high school diploma. I'm not proud of all the grades getting me there. Too many people want to throw the word racism around like it is a free pass for special privileges.

Looking at a few past events. I think it is important to address these as they were brought up as racial events of today. We will look at Michael Brown, and Trayvon Martin. Here we see two young Blacks killed by Whites.

Let's be honest viewing these individually. Michael Brown was black, and he was killed by a person that was white. This is a fact no one disputes. The reason for the interaction between the two persons were because he had allegedly been identified as having robbed a small store. This too appears not to be disputed. He was ordered to comply with the police officer, which he failed to do and was then shot as the two struggled.

This had nothing to do with race. This was about crime. Sure the famous Al Sharpton was quick to arrive and add more chaos while he filled his pockets with money and free publicity. People were bused in adding more turmoil. They screamed a young Black boy had been violently killed while his rights were violated. Where was Al Sharpton when it came to the store owner having his rights violated, by this same Black boy who was over six feet tall and three hundred plus pounds? The problem was the boy committed a crime.

The worst part, was the response of the community. They either purposely lied knowing that Michael Brown was defiant with the police officer, or they were ignorant in being led a stray before the facts and evidence could be gathered to solve the crime that had occurred.

I look at Ferguson Missouri as a perfect example of racism. Let us teach our children not to be accountable for their actions by screaming racism. In this case we have one dead child that can no longer contribute to his family, or his community. Is this not ignorant?

The community, along with those making a stand, are the true racist. They sacrificed the life of a child, not to mention the destruction of law-abiding citizens homes and businesses. These people cry and shout for peaceful restrain of police use of force, while they go out rob, loot, and burn their own church.

We will return to this, but let us move on to Trayvon Martin. Fact, he was Black, and was killed by someone who was reported White. The problem is that the shooter was not White; he was Hispanic. Here in this event the news media, flames the word racism as it helps bring in ratings. Our own President Obama jumped on the bandwagon, as he shouted to all Americans, that Trayvon Martin could have been his son, or could have been him. Was President Obama stating he was a trespasser at one time? I guess he did trespass in the Whitehouse if he was not legally proven to be an American citizen.

President Obama's actions made this crime an international incident. After these words were uttered, our country became more divided. We were divided by color, not just Black and White, but Blue. Our law enforcement branches were being targeted as police were being ambushed. President Obama basically gave a silent nod for Blacks to assault our police officers as he stood back watching from afar. He commented it was understandable their frustration. He was letting them know their actions were justified.

I look at racism like a scab on your arm. If you let it heal on its own, it will eventually vanish, but if you keep picking on it not letting it heal, then it will remain much longer. It may even leave scars that will never go away.

Racism must be viewed from all angles. Just look at the confederate flag. This is a part of our history, yet it offends a particular group of Black Americans. The next thing you know the flag gets banned from certain areas. Statutes of important Americans get removed from places that once honored these people as part of our history. We have Black history month in February; we have Cinco De Mayo in May, but where are the holidays for the Whites? Where are the all-White schools at? We have all-Black schools.

This is what has become known as reverse discrimination. We have some schools in Texas that refused to let their students wear their country's American Flag, yet they let the Mexican Flag fly freely and higher than ours.

As we identify racism, we must understand it is like an engine with many components. There are lots of components to racism. First, we can look at culturally.

Their beliefs, which involve their society and their way of living. This is part of their culture. If we look at their society, we will see it is different from ours. They believe that their neighborhoods belong only to them and that no one from outside that neighborhood should be allowed to enter without sacrificing their own safety.

Their society is more dangerous than anywhere else, due to the violence that they instill on others. Where does the violence come from? I have talked with many hundreds of citizens from these danger zones. Many view life as nothing of value.

They live for only today. Tomorrow to them is not in their schedule. One of their reasons are their families are broken up. Mom and dad have separated, leaving the kids too many times to fend for themselves. Dad wants nothing to do with the kids, for fear of child support. The mom is too busy working and the kids become shuffled goods. They grow up thinking school is not that important because they need money not knowledge.

These children grow up only focused on making money, not building a future. They will go out rob, sell drugs, whatever it takes to get the money that takes care of them and those around them. They lack in their communities good authority role models. Parents to start with, including teachers, ministers, police, and many more.

This leads us to crime, which is one of the biggest racial markers. President Obama talked to all of us as he stated, basically that a White person does not understand what it is like to walk across the street and hear a car door lock, or to be in a store and be watched by the employees who wonder if you are going to steal, or to see a woman clinch her purse after looking at her. Maybe he doesn't understand that not everyone has their own security detail that follow them around protecting them.

If you state that the Whites do not understand because they are White then know the Blacks do not understand because they are Black. We should be teaching about reality. The word accountability is often replaced by racism. Unfortunately former President Obama used racism to enable criminal behavior.

As we look at crime statistics, we must also know they may be presented in a manner that is true, but misleading. An article written by Khary Lazarre-White, titled Black on Black White on White violence. He states that In 2011, of the 12,664 murder victims in America, 50% were Black and 46% were white. In 2011, 52% of the offenders in these murders were Black and 45% were white. He mentioned 90% of the murders were by males.

While this may be true, could it tell us that we live our lives segregated? That Blacks live with Blacks and Whites live with Whites. It could be Blacks live in heavily populated cities and Whites live in more rural communities. These could certainly be interesting facts to explore.

The definition of poverty is, the state or condition of having little or no money, goods, or means of support; condition of being poor. I believe this is the key to racism. Khary identified himself as a gun control advocate. He mentioned he had spent every day for the last 18 years trying to reduce violence in Black and Latino communities. If this data he presented is true, why did he spend all that time in those communities, and not half the time in White communities, to add to his data unbiased?

I have yet to see a White community rebel after a Black police officer shoots a White suspect. I have not heard of any violent protests, or seen large groups of Whites destroying and looting their own communities. Those that looted during the Ferguson Riots were criminals. They used their race to conceal their true intent of criminal activity.

Those violating the curfew were only out to create chaos. Could they have had legitimate complaints about their law enforcement agency, it is very possible. The problem is that they chose to rob, steal, and loot, rather than address serious issues if that was their true reason for the riot.

Is it possible that these areas that are identified as very dangerous areas, places such as Chicago, Los Angeles, New York, and all the other big cities, is due not so much because these are heavily populated with Blacks, which they are, but with broken families that lack an educated community?

After the Ferguson Riots those that lived in that community talked with the news media. They just talked about getting back to work and getting everything back to normal. Was not normal the whole purpose of the riot. We're not these people upset with their treatment by law enforcement personnel? Were these people not upset with their own community destroying their own businesses? Why have no reporters covered this story since? Is this reality that we wish to forget?

The truth is the news agencies are owned by rich, powerful people that want the news to report only what they want us to know. They are looking at news not as reporting facts but covering stories that will entertain our minds keeping us curious for more. It is for getting their agenda out to us only.

Do I believe that Blacks have been racially targeted? I do believe they have been.

I think history speaks loudly that Blacks were originally not seen as an equal, valuable, knowledgeable, or civilized. It has taken time to get them to an equal status. Are they there yet? Not yet. This is because no one either wants to change, or things are put in play to make it look like we are helping them, while we really are enabling them.

We did bring Blacks over here as slaves. We did end up freeing them. They were freed not by Blacks, but by Whites that viewed them as more than property.

What if we clarify the Black and White perpetrators with a little more information so you will see a more realistic view of the data? We have an estimated population of 327,270,267 as of February 27, 2018, making the United States the third most populous country in the world.

There are approximately 231 million Whites in America, leaving 39 million Blacks, with 52 million Hispanics, yet it is the African Americans that lead in violence. In 2013 black males accounted for 37% of the total male prison population, white males 32%, and Hispanic males 22%. These numbers look close together until you look at the population total. If you look at both the African Americans and Hispanics, you see those numbers are high. Is this due to them being culturally different? Is this due to these areas are heavily soaked with criminal elements? I believe it is a combination of all this, including poor education, lack of good jobs, and a strong family support system. Can racism be turned around? I believe we can change.

I think in order to change racism, one must understand racism. Let's view this more closely If the market is high, who benefits? If the market is low, who benefits? Politicians are the benefactors as they try to unite us and divide us. It is a part of our history, north against the south, blacks against the whites, rich against the poor.

Our politicians look at Blacks as a commodity. They view the poor the same. They try to manipulate them through programs of special needs. The more you can keep the population dependent on the government the more they will comply to the governments' demands.

We have food stamps, free lunch programs at schools for those that need it. W.I.C. for women, infants, and children. Federal housing and assisted living programs. There are jobs, but mostly part time. The problem is no family can live on a part-time job income.

First, we need to become independent. This means while we may need assistance, we should not seek a long-term assistance from our government..

The African American fought hard to be heard as they now can vote. They fought hard to abolish segregation, yet they want to use this two ways. First, they want to be included in the white man's activities, while excluding them from some of theirs. Look at the all-white schools. Martin Luther King fought hard to end segregation, especially in the schools.

Most Americans view the African Americans of today as unappreciated people that think everything should be owed to them because of what their ancestors went through. Many view them as uncivilized as they demonstrate in the streets rioting, looting, fighting, jumping up and down like wild animals.

I believe that many things have been put in place to help not just the African Americans, but women, veterans, single women, and even atheists. While these groups receive extra points in obtaining jobs, they do take away from the whites merely on race itself. A qualified white male may be more qualified, yet is turned away because he is white and they need a Black, or a female. Is this not racism as well?

I am not looking to bring this up to throw stones, but rather to create an understanding to unite all races together. Like I had mentioned earlier look at Al Sharpton, President Obama, here we have two people that wish to represent the Black nation. They scream racism, when they ought to be screaming crime, corruption, poverty, and education.

While Martin Luther King had a dream, I have a plan. Though he was known, I am not. Listen to what my plan is and see if it makes sense. We can start small with a town like Ferguson, Missouri, or big with Chicago, Illinois.

First, we need to build the community. We need the community to encourage its people to work. I am not just talking about McDonald's, or other fast-food places.

I am talking businesses that are long termed that will hire employees giving them the financial stability they will need to live and survive on.

They need to build retirement packages that will encourage workers to want to stay for the long term. The communities need to eliminate the gangs by turning them in if they wish to maintain that same lifestyle.

This will be hard because we are talking about family members. No one wishes to turn on their family, but it will be needed to succeed. By eliminating gangs in your communities you will gain a sense of freedom that you have grown enslaved to. Let those in your communities know you are tough on crime. This will discourage criminals from wanting to be in your area.

IF you take those in gangs and give them a chance to be a productive citizen in their community by offering them respectable jobs, you will create a sense of self worth

We have got to push our children back in schools to get a good education. We need to educate our communities on how we communicate, so we do not seem ignorant and uncivilized when we try to express ourselves.

We should feel a sense of pride when we look around at our community. We should not feel threatened in our own neighborhoods by gangs, or thugs. If we build our communities from the inside working our way out to other communities, it will spread. The problem is simple, start with crime in your communities.

Eliminate gangs in your neighborhoods. This will take everybody working together.

When cleaning your house you always take out the garbage before you start sweeping. Building a community is the same way.

You first get rid of those that hurt your community by robbing, murdering, destroying, anything that harms your community. You then replace the things that need replaced and upgrade. Bringing in new jobs for employment. Bringing in malls and restaurants, schools, churches, even building your neighborhoods with new homes, parks, or just fixing up the old homes.

You then need to look at the adult role models that are available, starting with your parents. A strong family is one that has a strong foundation. The saying that blood is thicker than water is very real. Family loyalty is a must in rebuilding communities. The African American society should want white people to come and join in their neighborhoods. They should want them eating in their restaurants, using their streets and parks. They should want them learning right beside them in the school.

If we can learn to live together, we can segregate, not by color, but by good and bad. Let us segregate our bad apples and put them in a prison setting. Once they come out of prison their odds of re-offending will decrease because the criminal support system will be weaker while the community will be stronger, tolerating no criminal activity like before.

It will take time to build a strong community.

Like I was taught by my parents, and I preach to my children, it takes a lifetime to build a reputation and seconds to destroy one.

We already have established segregated communities within our borders. There are military bases including National Guard posts, prisons, work camps, boot camps, along with religious Mosques. We have segregated our rich and famous, Beverly Hills, Las Vegas strip, Miami, Florida, Hollywood, California, to the Slums and ghettos of Chicago, Los Angeles, and New York city, where many are jobless, uneducated, or lack positive motivation. We have the middle class who live modestly while working feverishly 40 to 60 hours weekly. Some work multiple jobs just trying to make ends meet.

We need our elected officials to stop throwing stones as they purposely try pointing fingers keeping us divided. It is in their best interest to keep us divided, to help them battle us, while making it look like they are on our side. The United States was founded on being united. It is what has made our country so powerful and respected.

At least I know and you know, that we have the potential to eliminate racism at any time, if we choose to. It just needs to be identified as not a racial issue, but rather a social issue. It is about how we are raised and if we will set high standards for our children. It is about trust, work ethic, integrity, loving one another. It is about building a safe community where our children can play outside with nothing to fear.

We must remember that racism is a two-way street. Racism will not change if we do not look at how it has affected White males. They have become racially discriminated against, making this reverse discrimination.

We need to bring back accountability, qualification, and opportunity fairly. We must remember that while the African Americans were brought here as cheap labor, classified as property, and abused inhumanely, that was then and this is now.

The Whites today did not do this. This was done a long time ago and White males are paying for it now.

We have given them their freedom back. The blacks can vote, go to schools and receive a good education. They receive jobs merely on being black, often times taking a job away from a more skilled worker. We need to remember if they won't stop hating white people for what happened in the past, then they are the ones feeding racism. It is the blacks that are making the whites of today hate them, merely because they blame us for something we had no control over.

Let us not forget that our political leaders more often than not represent the minority rather than the majority. The minority is Washington's political circle. We can eliminate racism by uniting together as Americans. We can rid racism by fighting hard on crime, erasing poverty by building strong long-term jobs with retirement packages, keeping families together with both parents.

America it is up to us to work together and view each other as important. United we stand, divided we fall.

While I believe my ideas are good, it will take leaders that are known to make it happen. Those leaders in those communities must encourage their residents to want to change. They need to get them to trust and believe it can happen.

Strong people who lead with confidence can make a difference. Martin Luther King was one man. He was a great leader. He had millions follow him. Martin Luther King had a dream, and he wasn't afraid to share it. We need that type of leader again.

I believe most people want to be judged on their own merits. They want to be given a fair chance, not judged from their outside looking in, but from their inside looking out. If Whites are blamed for what our ancestors did then we too are being judged.

Where does racism stop? Who will say enough is enough? We need to open our eyes. Racism will end when we separate it from criminal behavior. When we create a fair and qualified system of hiring and firing,. We need to identify poverty in with racism, building torn run down dangerous communities back up into nice respected safe communities. We need to build single families whole again. Children deserve to live growing up with both parents in a loving environment.

The ink is black the page is white, together we can all again unite.

Martin Luther King Jr.

A great Black leader that wanted to bring equality to all while uniting us rather than divide us.

Malcolm X

A Black leader that was great at dividing us, Black verses White. He was more about Black power than equality.

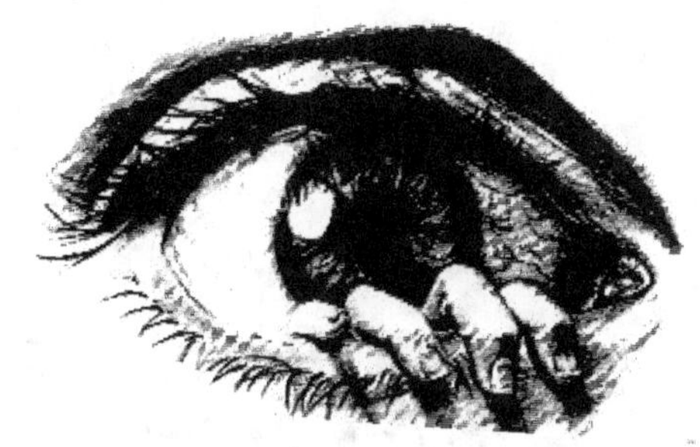

EDUCATION
EDUCATING THE IGNORANT

It is time to raise our hands and ask questions. Has our education system gotten better, or worse? Do our teachers still meet the high standards they once did? Are the teachers still teaching as much, or are they just sending the school work home for the children's parents to get done?

Do our teachers know how to teach? Is there a separation between the school faculties and the student's parents? As we cover educaton, we will get into lots of areas that will have you shaking your head. Let us start off with basic math. Here we will look at a common core math and what it is.

Common Core math

"old fashion" way

32

-12

20

The "New" way

32-12= _______

12 + 3 = 15
15 + 5 = 20
20 + 10 = 30
30 + 2 = 32
20 ← Answer

Does this image not look more complicated than the old fashioned way? To me it is like teaching a child to read before he knows how to spell the words he is reading. What happened to the simple problem. You have 32 apples and you take away 12 how many do you have?

Here is another example of a common core problem. As we look at this problem, understand they want to know what 6+9 =. As they explain the process, the first thing they ask is what plus 6 = 10? It is 4. Then they ask 4+? = 9? The answer is 5. You then add the 4 with the 6 which gives you 10. Then you add the 5 to get fifteen. I look at this question and ask Why do you need to turn the 6 in to a 10? Are they not making a simple problem hard? Was the way we did math 40, or 50 years ago that bad?

While I understand learning better ways is never a bad thing. We must ask if this formula is even beneficial? Let's not forget what the question was asking. It Was asking what 6+9= it wanted the answer 15. There is no number 10 in the problem, they added that creating more questions for the students.

In another curricular, such as language arts. It appears common core makes sense as they create sentences with realistic choices. So while it may be good for one class it may not be for another class. The problem is that it is designed to sell to schools as a bundle. You buy it like you do your television cable. You may want certain channels, but to get those channels you have to buy channels you really don't want, or know you won't watch.

History has always been an important class, and the foundation of learning who we are. As we look at the Civil War as an example. We see according to Wikipedia, the Civil War was a war against slavery. It was from 1861 to 1865.

However, Republican Board member, Pat Hardy stated that slavery was a side issue in the Civil War. She states it was over a state's rights.

In Texas 5 million students in public schools will begin to use new social studies textbooks based on the states academic standards that barely address racial segregation. The state's guideline for teaching American history do not mention the Ku Klux Klan, or Jim Crow Laws.

The children are to learn the conflict was caused by sectionalism, states' rights and slavery. Written deliberately in that order to telegraph slavery's secondary role in driving the conflict, according to some members of the state board of education. This is a perfect example of reprograming our students through education. The Jim Crow Laws were state and local laws that enforced racial segregation in the Southern United States.

They were enacted by White Democratic- dominated state legislatures in the late 19th century. These laws continued to be enforced until 1965.

The Ku Klux Klan, also known as KKK, or the Klan, refers to three distinct secret movements at different points of time in the United States.

The first Klan flourished in the Southern United States in the late 1860s. It sought to overthrow the Republican state governments in the South during the Reconstruction years. They used violence against African American leaders. It died out by the early 1870s.

The second group was founded in 1915 in the South. They flourished nationwide in the early and mid-1920s. This included areas of the Midwest and west This Klan used marketing techniques and a popular fraternal organization structure. It was rooted in local protestant communities. It sought to maintain White supremacy. They opposed Catholics and Jews and took a pro-prohibition stance.

The third group emerged after 1950 in localized and isolated groups that used the KKK name.

They focused on the opposition to the civil rights movement. They often used violence including murder to suppress activists. They are classified as a hate group by the Anti-Defamation League, and the Southern Poverty Law Center. Is this being taken out of our history books, because we do not want to offend anyone? Is this not who we once were? Are we so ashamed of ourselves we have to change our history showing only our good times?

Republican Board member, Pat Hardy and others like her, talk about slavery was not a primary reason for the war. If this is true then why do they associate the confederate flag with racism? Should it not be defined as sectionalism?

A flag from our past

What comes to your mind when viewing the flag? I see the South against the North. I see during this time period The South fighting to maintain slavery. Through Hollywood it has been viewed as a rebel flag.

The show Dukes of Hazzard comes to mind as they have a rebel flag on their car. They try to portray the police as corrupt while they are the innocent ones being framed and taken advantage of.

Above is the battle flag used by General Robert E. Lee. In war we must remember, in order to win, one must lose. Are we to ignore our history, or discard pieces of it due to possibly offending someone? As we observe events unfolding, how will our education system respond? The confederate statues are at war as they try to preserve a place in history for what was their time.

All four of the Confederate Soldiers and Sailors Monument on Mount Royal Avenue, the Confederate Women's Monument on West University Parkway, the Roger B. Taney Monument on Mount Vernon Place and the Robert E. Lee and Thomas. J. "Stonewall" Jackson Monument in the Wyman Park Dell — have been removed.

Why are the teachers and the education department not fighting to maintain a piece of our history? Stonewall Jackson is described as one of the best known Confederate Commanders after General Robert E. Lee. He played a prominent role in almost all the military engagements in the Eastern theater of the war until his death.

Roger B. Taney was the author of the infamous Dred Scott Decision. The Dred Scott case was a landmark decision by the United States Supreme Court on US labor law and constitutional law. It held that a negro whose ancestors were imported into and sold as slaves whether enslaved or free could not be an American citizen and therefore had no standing to sue in federal court. The decision was only the second time that the Supreme Court had ruled an act of congress to be unconstitutional.

The Women's monument on West University Parkway represents the women in military service for America memorial. It was established by the U.S. federal government which honors women who have served in our United States Armed Forces. It is located at the entrance of Arlington National Cemetery. As we view these, think about our history that has been destroyed. The Confederate Soldiers and Sailors Monument was installed in Baltimore, Maryland. The Maryland Daughters of the Confederacy raised money for the monument privately and commissioned a sculptor from New York city. The statue shows Glory supporting a fallen soldier, his standard lowered but her wreath of History held high. The inscription at the base of the monument read, "GLORIA VICTIS", meaning "Glory to the Vanquished.

The monument was defaced in June 2015, with "black lives matter" scrawled across its side in the aftermath of the Charleston church shooting. The Black Lives Matter organization should be identified as a hate group.

This is a piece of our history. It has been destroyed. Many may not like what they stood for, we are here today because of them. The South lost, and the North won. We should all be grateful, not forgetful. Everything that has happened in our time and before us, has directed us to where we are today. President Obama is to blame for this as he has reignited racism while he was in office.

What if we left those statues? We could put up new ones beside the old, showing leaders that have concord tyranny? Why not show we are survivors, not victims? Would this not show new leaders among these old ones and show how we have progressed?

When you look back at certain Super Bowl games, they always mention two teams. They do this knowing only one team one and the other lost. When we learned to ride a bike, we didn't forget the times we failed, often tipping over, or crashing on the side of the road. As we leave history a moment and travel back to the present, we observe our colleges.

Our colleges have turned from learning environments, into political battlefields. Conservatives becoming victims by the Liberals. Colleges were designed to educate our students in a friendly and unbiased manner.

The professors have always been persons of strong belief, however a good professor enjoys debate and challenging his students on both sides. He is comfortable allowing both sides to walk away winners, or if only one then to at least not make the other side feel hated, or threatened. Let's review a few events.

Bryan Stascavage wrote an article in the Wesleyan University paper. He also did two tours in the Iraq war. Bryan was doing an article on the Black Lives Matter movement. The student activists did not like his way of thinking and targeted him. They stole hundreds of papers with his article in them burning and shredding them. He was called racist and the student activist put pressure on the administrators to de-fund the campus paper.

Aryssa Damron, a sophomore student at Yale has been called a bigot and was harassed for her beliefs. She wears the Republican apparel items like the elephant or other stickers or pins identifying herself as a conservative. One student had told her that she could not live with her because she was too conservative.

She stated that she is searching for the open mindedness on her campus, but that it is a very liberal campus and city. She mentioned conservatives on campus are often minimized. Aryssa stated she loved Yale and what the name can bring to students, but would not want her kids to go there. If it is not good enough for your kids then why wear the Yale title with pride? I think she is saying graduating Yale makes her somebody above the rest?

Members of the LGBT community at Missouri State University are demanding the school retaliate against a student leader for her off-campus activism against a local ordinance that could harm religious freedom. Lindsey Kolb, supported the repeal of a city ordinance that band discrimination, based on sexual orientation and gender. She argued it did not provide substantial religious exemptions for businesses and individuals. She did this on her time. She was away from campus. It appears members of the LGBT are pushing to silence her from her first amendment right that being the freedom of speech. If Congress can't make laws due to the Constitution, which protects establishments freedom to exercise their religious rights, how can the LGBT realistically expect too? This group would scream if the roles were reversed. They expect all their rights to be preserved while attacking everyone else's.

Jonathan Zhao, was a student member at Duke University who wrote conservative articles. On one of his articles he stated the Black community was its own worst enemy. He was savagely smeared as the students petitioned for the Chronicle to fire him.

They had a banner that stated, "We do not believe students have a protected right to use a student publication as a platform to proliferate racist stereotypes and misinformation."

A political science professor used her syllabi to ask students "to write and speak in a way that does not assume American-ness, maleness, whiteness, heterosexuality, middle-class status, etc. to be the norm." The student felt judged before the class had even started.

It sounds to me like they are describing a White middle class working man. They want you to think like either a woman, African American, or Immigrant.

Anything but what you may be if you are male and White and are of middle-class origins. Have our colleges gone too far pushing their Liberal views on those that have chosen to remain Conservative?

They can say these are just a few examples, and they don't reflect the rest of the colleges and their ways of thinking. The colleges haven't condoned, the behavior against Conservatives, or Republicans. There is also the point that the Liberal student activists had to have been directed, inspired, or taught from someone. Where did they get their views? Why do they express themselves through violence, intimidation, and total disregard for other human's rights and values?

Going back to October 1995. The First Circuit ruled, in *Brown v. Hot, Sexy and Safer Productions,* Inc., parents do not have a "fundamental constitutional right to dictate the curriculum [or assessments] at the public school to which they have chosen to send their children. The courts stated that you give up your rights when you send them to a public school willingly. You do not have to send them to a public school. You can send them to a private or home school them.

In this particular case The plaintiffs are two minors and their parents. The minors allege that they were compelled to attend an indecent AIDS and sex education program conducted at their public high school by defendant Hot, Sexy and Safer Productions "Hot, Sexy, and Safer". ☐

Plaintiffs allege, inter alia, that the compelled attendance deprived the minors of their privacy rights and they're right to an educational environment free from sexual harassment. ☐ The district court granted the defendants' motion to dismiss under Federal Rule of Civil Procedure 12(b)(6). ☐ We affirm.

Plaintiffs allege that Landolphi gave sexually explicit monologues and participated in sexually suggestive skits with several minors chosen from the audience. ☐ Specifically, the complaint alleges that Landolphi: 1) told the students that they were going to have a "group sexual experience, with audience participation"; 2) used profane, lewd, and lascivious language to describe body parts and excretory functions; 3) advocated and approved oral sex, masturbation, homosexual sexual activity, and condom use during promiscuous premarital sex; 4) simulated masturbation; 5) characterized the loose pants worn by one minor as "erection wear"; 6) referred to being in "deep sh--" after anal sex; 7) had a male minor lick an oversized condom with her, after which she had a female minor pull it over the male minor's entire head and blow it up; 8) encouraged a male minor to display his "orgasm face" with her for the camera; 9) informed a male minor that he was not having enough orgasms; 10) closely inspected a minor and told him he had a "nice butt"; and 11) made eighteen references to orgasms, six references to male genitals, and eight references to female genitals.

This information came from the following link. https://caselaw.findlaw.com/us-1st-circuit/1014792.html. Does this not seem like over kill? Remember we are talking about high school students.

Are we not able to communicate and teach without crossing into lewd and lascivious behavior? A child that grows up with strong Christian values could be offended by this form of theatrics.

Let us look at boundaries in the schools In the Ultraviolet Marlborough school student newspaper, they reported that Lauren had a falling out with her close friend over the summer. Upon her return she was asked through emails how she was doing? Teachers began watching her closer which brought unwanted attention from the other students who gossiped. The Head of Upper School and Assistant Head of School Laura Hotchkiss explained that when student issues arise, they are always handled by her and School Counselor Emily Vaughn. When Hotchkiss and Vaughn perceive a noticeable change in a student's emotional state or physical appearance, they either contact the student directly or arrange a meeting with the student's parents to discuss the perceived problem.

School administrators try to make sure that every student feels part of a nurturing environment that provides appropriate help and support.

Once a student and their parents tell [the faculty] that their assistance is not needed or wanted, they continue to force involvement, which feels really invasive, according to one of the students. I understand teaching can be hard work, but there are lines, and boundaries where a teacher should be teaching and not parenting. It is good that they care enough for the students, but bring the concerns to the parents and take their guidance.

We will cover some interesting stories that really happened. It is stories like these that give schools a bad name. I often think of how one bad cop can make a whole department look bad.

One parent stated that her kids were scheduled with Friday and a Monday off from school. She was taking her kids to North Carolina for a visit with family members. They would not get back till late Tuesday, so they would miss a day of school. She stated her daughter had only missed one day of school, and her other daughter had missed five due to pneumonia. She said the school called her to explain the importance of attendance. She told them she was not interested in hearing that, due to her children hardly ever missed. Her one child that missed five days was all together due to pneumonia.

The school sent a form for them to fill out highlighting in pink that unless the day was a learning experience that it would not be accepted as a legal day off.

I think they mentioned the school had a zero tolerance on attendance. Common sense would tell you, things come up from sickness, deaths, to actual vacations where parents have to take a vacation during the school year due to low seniority. Jobs like, correctional officers, police, nurses, and other first responders. Not everyone can be off together. Someone has to watch the prisoners. Let's not forget the word reality. How many teachers have worked any job outside of a school setting? They graduated high school, went to college then back in full time in to the schools as teachers. Their bosses are principles and Deans.

Teachers have taken on the role of teaching and preaching, often not listening to no one who is degreeless. This by itself teaches our students not to listen to parents and presents the teachers as above the rest.

The problem is that teachers are to be teaching our kids responsibility, respect, and accountability.

Our world is constantly changing. Things that were ok, no more are. Zac Wells, a Merrillville's veteran football coach talked about boundaries. That it is just common sense to keep safe professional distances between the adult teachers, staff and the students. In today's world, there are no more one-on-one session with teachers and students behind closed doors. That no teacher should drive a child home alone after school without another adult present.

You have to be careful what you say, keeping your personal life separate, so as it can't be construed in the wrong context.

Several coaches said that high school girls are more daring, not thinking twice about flirting with a teacher. It takes a lifetime to build a reputation and a second to destroy one. You need to be aware of your surroundings, never putting yourself in an area of questionability. Unfortunately, this is our world. This does bring in additional situations that we all will view differently. Kids will be kids and they can be mean to one another. While we pressure teachers to teach and not to parent, we have to understand some kids will need discipline. Who does the discipline? The parents that may or may not see their child guilty? The teachers who will be seen as overstepping their boundaries? It comes down to both working together.

As we continue on looking at today's school environment, we see there are many issues that have remained throughout our history.

Some of these issues are teen hormones, finding their identity, becoming independent, along with just rebelling against authority. While these continue to challenge us, other issues arise in the form of technology. Kids have phones with them as they are in class to study. These phones temporarily cause the kids to lose focus as they talk with others when they should be studying.

They use other programs out there like Snap Chat, Instant Graham, ICQ, Myspace, Email, Twitter, and Facebook. Here students have no escape. Here they become sometimes victims, or possibly famous in their own virtual world. Often living life more online than in the present with friends and family who beg to support them.

Here the teachers can monitor their students as well if they are friends on any of the online sites. Bullying has always been a problem in school, but now they have Cyber bullying, which makes the bully sometimes unidentifiable. Suicides have gone up, sometimes due to the overwhelming mass audiences. On line you are just one click away from being a target.

The internet gives the children quick access to all types of information without them having to search the old fashioned way through textbooks. This may be quicker, but takes away reading and comprehending. The final area we will address is social time, along with peer pressure.

One of the biggest arguments on public school verse home schooling, is that you take the children out of the environment that teaches them social skills. These are important skills you need to be able to communicate and interact with your peers. I know some kids will have a harder time than others, but those are the kids that will define themselves as survivors, leaders, followers, or victims.

I can say I had a hard time in school, but I did not quit, I became a Marine, Counselor, Correctional Officer, Parent, and Grandparent. I pushed myself harder to achieve what came easy to others. I am not upset with my classmates. They help me become who I am today.

Every child out there has potential. Some teachers are good at bringing that potential out while others are good at helping you keep it in. If we take away our children's calculators how many could add, subtract, multiply, and divide?

How many could find battles in our history books without texting on Google?

We are only as smart as our teachers, our parents, our politicians that try swaying our young generation. Where will our educators go from here? I think common sense will direct us to work together if we wish to educate our students productively.

GUNS IN AMERICA
FIGHTING FOR OUR FREEDOM

America has always been a great nation. We have overcome much. We became an independent country in 1776. Having won our independence through countless battles. Our country was formed by the use of the gun. It has been one of our greatest protectors.

The Second Amendment states, a well-regulated Militia, being necessary to the security of a free state, the right of the people to keep and bear Arms, shall not be infringed. This is important still to us all. The Constitution was designed to protect us from enemies, both foreign and domestic. We must not forget those men of all ages that grabbed their guns in the night and charged for our freedom. We called them Minute Men. Today they would be called National Guardsmen, Army Reserve, Marine Reserve, Coast Guard, and Air National

Guard.

Many members of our families have already served in one of our branches of military. Those that have not, are still Americans. They have the same rights. They have the same constitutional rights as everyone else. Our gun rights have been the center of controversy a long time. Our great politicians have used guns for their own agenda in getting elected in to office. There are two groups, each divided when it comes to guns. Those that support guns and those that oppose them. We will cover both sides and listen to their arguments.

Looking first at those that oppose guns. This group believes there should be gun control through firearms regulation. This is a set of laws and policies that regulate the manufacture, sale, transfer, possession, modification, and storage of firearms. Let's not forget the use of firearms by civilians.

The first person I will introduce is U.S. Congresswoman Nancy Pelosi, also Speaker of the House. She is all about gun control She voted no, on prohibiting product misuse lawsuits on gun manufacturers. A bill to prohibit civil liability actions from being brought or continued against manufacturers, distributors, dealers, or importers of firearms or ammunition for damages, injunctive or other relief resulting from the misuse of their products by others.

A yes vote would Prohibit individuals from filing a qualified civil liability action. Exempt lawsuits brought against individuals who knowingly transfer a firearm that will be used to commit a violent or drug-trafficking crime.

Exempt lawsuits against actions that result in death, physical injury or property damage due solely to a product defect.

Dismiss of all civil liability actions pending on the date of enactment.

Prohibit the manufacture, import, sale or delivery of armor piercing ammunition.

Nancy Pelosi voted no, on decreasing gun waiting time from 3 days to 1 day.

Gun activist scream that crime is worse due to all the guns out there. They state, better gun control would take the guns from the criminals. They want us to believe that guns push us into killing one another. All the killings that have taken place on the streets and in the schools, such as the Columbine High School shooting, Sandy Hook shooting, The Batman Theater shooting, and thousands more are due to the guns and not the shooters behind the gun.

As we continue, we will review the statistics to see if what they say is true. These politicians forget to mention many of them carry guns, or have someone nearby with a gun for their protection. Nancy Pelosi may just be one politician, but she is highly respected among her colleagues as she is Speaker of the House.

She is just one of many politicians that wish to take our rights away when it comes to our gun rights and Second Amendment.

The spokesman for the Chicago Police Department, Anthony Guglielmi, blamed the numbers on gang conflicts driven partly due to social media commentary and petty disputes among rival factions. He called for more crackdowns on guns, stating every year Chicago Police recover more illegal guns than any officers in any other city. He pointed out that illegal guns find their way into their neighborhoods. Anthony Guglielmi stated it is clear we need stronger state and federal gun laws.

In 2015 almost 3,000 people in Chicago were shot. There were 31 wounded and 9 killed at this time last year. The statistics were last recorded this high, in 2012. It is interesting that the President of the United States at that time was Barack Obama. He also wanted to classify himself as an African American.

One site that keeps track of Chicago violence reported that 81.8 percent of homicide victims in 2016 had been black and 90 percent had been male. As we look at some of Chicago's most recent statistics, remember this was one of the city's with the strictest gun laws.

Today is June 7, 2018. Just in this month there have been 7 shot and killed, 49 shot and wounded. That is a total of 56 people, with 7 of them being classified homicides. Since the beginning of the year we have had 178 shot and killed, 927 shot and wounded, making a total of 1105, with 213 as the ending count in homicides.

The deadliest neighborhoods in Chicago

Neighborhood	Homicides	Wounded	Total
Austin	32	120	152
Garfield Park	16	88	104
Englewood	14	55	69
North Lawndale	12	52	64
Humboldt Park	9	54	63
Grand Crossing	4	38	42
New City	10	30	40
Little Village	3	36	39
Auburn Gresham	7	27	34
West Pullman	10	23	33
Chatham	10	21	31
Chicago Lawn	8	22	30
South Shore	8	22	30
Near West Side	3	24	27
Roseland	3	21	24
All Others	64	289	353

The statistics tell us a lot. The spokesman for the Chicago Police Department, Anthony Guglielmi, stated that the police in Chicago had recovered more illegal guns than any other city. The key word is illegal guns. Most of them were either stolen or modified. Our politicians cry for more gun control, yet Chicago is the perfect example of, tried it and it didn't work. On the other page you can view neighborhoods not to enter. This is not due to guns this is due to poverty, education, and a lack of parenting and adult role models. The combination of all these infest neighborhoods into crime. Before you take away law abiding gun owner's rights, lets clean up the criminal elements one by one.

Let's look at New York City and their statistics.

In New York, annual deaths resulting from firearms total

2014: 875
2013: 863
2012: 977
2011: 997
2010: 1,011
2009: 958
2008: 963
2007: 985
2006: 1,002
2005: 1,019
2004: 951
2003: 1,034
2002: 994
2001: 1,068
2000: 1,093
1999: 1,016

In New York, civilians are not allowed to possess machine guns, assault weapons and large capacity ammunition magazines with few exceptions, but civilians are allowed to possess.50 caliber rifles. In New York, private possession of semi-automatic assault weapons is prohibited with only narrow exemptions. In New York, private guns are prohibited in state parks, child care facilities, state-operated mental health facilities, New York City (with limited exceptions), vehicles universities and schools.

It appears they are really saying you cannot own a gun in New York City. Let us move on to another city that has a bad reputation for crime, Washington D.C. In Washington D.C. their gun ban worsened the city's homicide rate.

In 1976, D.C. implemented a law that banned citizens from owning guns, as only police officers were allowed to carry firearms. Those who already owned guns were allowed to keep them only if they were disassembled or trigger-locked. Trigger locks could only be removed if the owner received permission from the D.C. police, which was rare.

Annual homicides rose from 188 in 1976 to 364 in 1988 and then increased even further to 454 in 1993. The gun ban was struck down by the Supreme Court in District of Columbia vs. Heller, and homicides have steadily declined since then to 88 yearly murders in 2012. The statistics clearly show that crime rose more during the strict gun ban and declined when the Supreme Court ruled it unconstitutional. Why do we continue to argue when the evidence shows different?

The criminals thrive in areas where gun restrictions are high. The vast majority of mass shootings occur in gun free zones. The Crime Research Prevention Center determined that since 1950 nearly 99 percent of mass shootings have occurred in gun free zones. The terror attack in Orlando Florida, the shooting that took the life of Christina Grimmie in June, the Sandy hook and countless other school shootings all took place in gun free zones.

It is obvious that these killers thrive on the helpless. Anyone with common sense can see this. One of the biggest arguments for pro-gun owners and activist is this reason. It's our right to protect a person, place, or thing. This is our constitutional right. Predators don't go into police stations where there are tons of guns to kill, or on military bases where they will clearly be outnumbered and outmatched.

We supposedly have 320 million people in our country yet only 628,000 police officers. The police cannot be everywhere. They depend on us to assist them as law-abiding citizens, witnesses. We are law-abiding citizens with rights. We have the right to protect ourselves and belongings. We have the constitution of the United States the supreme law of the land, which is just under God. Guns are for protection, but survival too. We use guns to hunt. There are all kind of game we hunt annually. It is for family time as well.

I grew up owning a 22 rifle and shooting a 12-gauge shotgun, strictly for hunting and target practice. I was taught gun safety by my dad. I can't imagine living in a state that would violate your constitutional rights, by people who themselves carry guns or have gun protection. Our politicians so often forget who put them in office, or who they are there to serve.

Protection for these days is a must. Some people's only protection may be the gun. A woman home alone has a choice, grab the phone, or grab the gun. Should they call 911 in hopes someone will get there in time to protect them, or grab the gun and protect them self immediately and call 911 when they can get to the phone safely? She did not ask for them to come rob, rape, or intend to murder her. We have been taught to be survivors, not victims.

We have training for law-abiding citizens that wish to carry conceal weapons. With some laws out there, even the conceal carry persons are limited to where they can travel. These are areas called gun free zones, or what I call areas of opportunity to the predators. The statistics show more crime happens in these safe zones than in areas where guns are allowed.

You could look at California as a safe zone state. There are areas in California that are pro-gun and due not concur with the rest of the state. In California there were 1,930 murders, 13,702 rapes, 54,789 robberies, and 104,375 assaults. They stated on the website you had a chance of 1 in 225 of becoming a victim of a violent assault. This was on, https://www.neighborhoodscout.com/ca/crime

Those on the left often point to Australia and Great Britain as success stories in gun control while the evidence does just the opposite. The Crime Research Prevention Center found in Great Britain's case that. After the gun ban was implemented, that the homicide rate rose immensely, and only decreased slightly once Great Britain's law enforcement agency was increased.

I think we have shown pretty consistently that, guns influence the criminals in where they target their victims. They continue to target defenseless victims. Anyone with any common sense is going to choose a victim that isn't armed, verses one that is.

As we move on, we will look at what the statistics show in regard to the American view on gun ownership. Are we to believe these charts, graphs, and editorial comments that may be bought and paid for by the left?

I do believe that we do have two groups of gun thinking people, those that think guns are dangerous and kill innocent victims way too often. The other group believe that guns don't kill by themselves. They believe that it is the shooter and his mind that chose whether to harm others. They believe that the shooter should be held accountable for his actions and not blame the killing on the gun.

Let us look at this chart on the next page. It came from, http://www.pewresearch.org/fact-tank/2017/06/22/key-takeaways-on-americans-views-of-guns-and-gun-ownership/

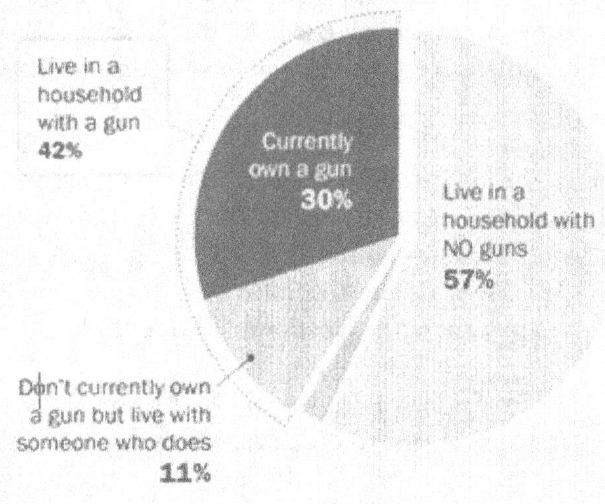

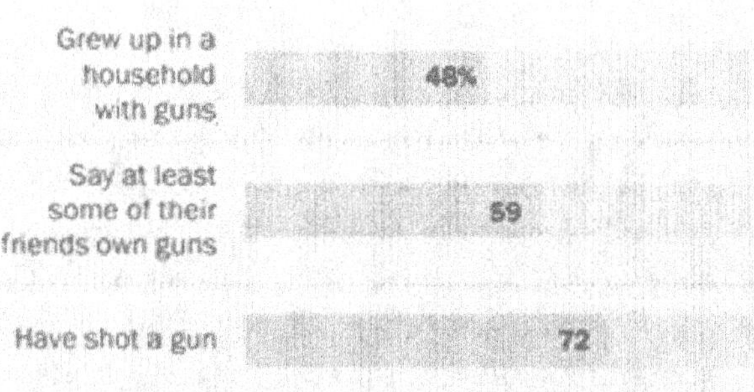

Note: In pie chart, share of respondents who didn't offer an answer shown but not labeled. Figures may not add to 100% or to subtotals indicated due to rounding.
Source: Survey of U.S. adults conducted March 13-27 and April 4-18, 2017.
'America's Complex Relationship With Guns'
PEW RESEARCH CENTER

U.S. Air Force

U.S. Marines

U.S. Army

U.S. Navy

U.S. Coast Guard

U.S. Space Force

Our country has a reputation of being armed and ready.

This does not hold to just our military, but our millions of American residences who pride themselves on gun ownership. The chart on the other page reflects that only 30 percent own guns. This information, while honestly recorded is misleading. They state that 57 percent do not live in homes with guns.

If I were called to partake in this data, I would not tell them I have guns either. Do I own guns? Maybe? How many guns? I would never say. Those that believe in their second Amendment, know that this data could be collected and used at a later time if we were ever to go into a martial law type situation. Preventing our military from snatching and grabbing guns like what has been done in other countries. That's like receiving a map with directions to every gun-owners home.

You must be open to the data that is received knowing these are reasons why it will not show truth, but deception. Gun owners want to speak out, without putting themselves at risk down the road. Gun owners understand that the constitution protects them from a corrupt government.

We have the Executive branch, Legislative branch, and Judicial branch. They keep the other in check and balance. The Constitution is there to protect the people's rights. Politicians will spin the words of any document to fit their agenda. The constitution's 2nd Amendment A well-regulated Militia, being necessary to the security of a free state, the right of the people to keep and bear Arms, shall not be infringed. Try spinning this.

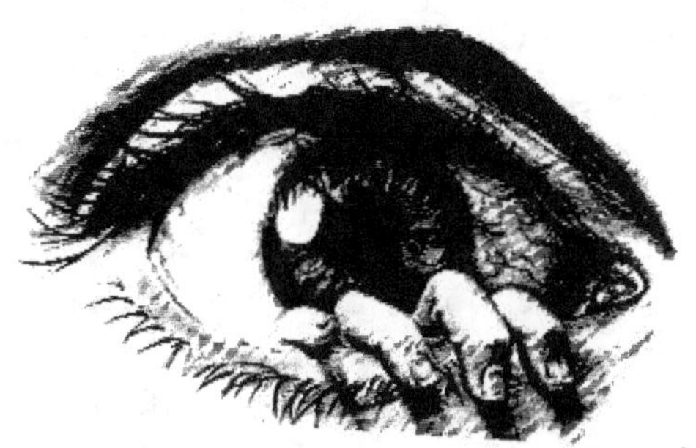

EXECUTIVE ORDERS
TRUE LEADERSHIP

As we head into this next chapter, we will look at What President Donald Trump has accomplished. There are all types of leaders out there, but he has not only woken our sleeping politicians, but challenged those at the helm who seek to run their own elite agendas, ignoring what we the people want. Ignoring those that have put them in office to represent us.

President Donald Trump ran for president to help make America great again. Is he doing it? Is he meeting resistance? Are those that voted him in disappointed? Can one man take on Washington? Come with me as we explore firsthand. America is becoming what it once was, a proud nation feared and respected by all.
President Trump first started off running for this Office of the President of the United States.

He came in with a loud roar. He stated we need to be thinking about trade deals with China, Japan, India, with everybody. We are getting ripped apart piece by piece slowly. The president stated that China laughs at us, at our stupidity. He mentioned he loved the Mexican people, and respects Mexico as a country. His problem is that they are much smarter, much sharper, and much more cunning than our leaders. He talked about immigration and securing the border by building a wall.

He addressed Common Core. He has stated he was not going to take money from lobbyist and special interest groups. He talked about taxes being lowered and even getting rid of the I.R.S. He has focused on building the economy by bringing jobs back to America, or taxing those companies that took their business outside of our borders.

President Trump has taken on racism and stood tall for our men in blue who go out every day fighting to keep our cities and streets safe from the criminal elements. He has been pushed away by some of his close friends when he started his campaign. Then he has had to deal with the media that was viciously bias, editing almost everything he said to tarnish him. A normal man would have given up, but he pushed back challenging those that altered the truth. He exposed them for who they were.

I want you to be aware of this as we go through his accomplishments. I want you to know he has been attacked by all sides with only the support of us common people The American deplorable, which I stand proudly as.

On January 20, 2017, President Donald Trump signs his first executive order. **Executive Order 13765.** The order was designed to weaken regulations and procedures associated with enforcement of the Patient Protection and Affordable Care Act. The executive order was to end Obama Care.

Executive Order 13766 was signed on January 24, 2017. this order establishes a new system by which to fast-track the construction of infrastructure projects.

Executive Order 13767 Border Security and Immigration Enforcement Improvements. Was signed on January 25, 2017. The order directs "executive departments and agencies to deploy all lawful means to secure the Nation's southern border, to prevent further illegal immigration into the United States, and to repatriate illegal aliens swiftly, consistently, and humanely", and states that "It is the policy of the executive branch to secure the southern border of the United States through the immediate construction of a physical wall on the southern border.

Executive Order 13768 Enhancing Public Safety in the interior of the United States. This order was signed on January 25, 2017. The order stated that "sanctuary jurisdictions" including "sanctuary_cities" who refused to comply with immigration enforcement measures would not be "eligible to receive Federal grants, except as deemed necessary for law enforcement purposes" by the U.S. Attorney General or Secretary of Homeland Security. In just five days in office the president signed 4 Executive Orders, covering healthcare, infrastructure, border security, and security from within our borders.

Executive Order 13769 Protecting the Nation from Foreign Terrorist Entry into the United States. It is also known as the Muslim Ban, or Travel Ban. It lowered the number of refugees to be admitted into the United States in 2017 to 50,000, suspended the U.S. Refugee Admissions Program (USRAP) for 120 days, suspended the entry of Syrian refugees indefinitely, directed some cabinet secretaries to suspend entry of those whose countries do not meet adjudication standards under U.S. immigration law for 90 days, and included exceptions on a case-by-case basis. Homeland Security lists these countries as Iran, Iraq, Libya, Somalia, Sudan, Syria, and Yemen. Executive Order 13769 was a temporary order that was blocked by various courts. It was in effect from January 27, 2017 to March 16, 2017.

Executive Order 13770 Ethics Commitments by Executive Branch Employees. This was a contract put in place to ensure that those in the Executive Branch that were employed, conducted themselves professionally. It held them accountable for their actions while in office and for up to five years after office. This order was signed on January 28, 2017.

Executive Order 13771 Reducing Regulation and controlling Regulatory Costs. This was signed on January 30, 2017. It directs agencies to repeal two existing regulations for every new regulation, and to do so in such a way that the total cost of regulations does not increase. This was to help reduce all the excessive regulations that were in place. President Trump's first month in office he signs 7 Executive Orders.

Executive Order 13772 Core Principals for Regulating the United States Financial System. This order was signed on February 3, 2017. It established the core principles of regulation under the Trump administration and tasked the United States Department of Treasury to review the Financial Stability Oversight Council. It was originally formed under the Dodd-Frank Wall Street Reform and Consumer Protection Act and report to the President in 120 days on current regulations and their effectiveness in carrying out these core principles.

Executive Order 13773 Enforcing Federal Law with Respect to Transnational Criminal Organizations and Preventing International Trafficking. This was signed on February 9, 2017. This was to strengthen enforcement of Federal law in order to thwart transnational criminal organizations and subsidiary organizations, including criminal gangs, cartels, racketeering organizations, and other groups engaged in illicit activities that present a threat to public safety and national security and that are related, such as the illegal smuggling and trafficking of humans, drugs or other substances, wildlife, and weapons corruption, Cybercrime, fraud, financial crimes, and intellectual-property theft; or the illegal concealment or transfer of proceeds derived from such illicit activities.

Executive Order 13774 Preventing Violence Against Federal, State, Tribal, and Local Law Enforcement Officers. This was signed on February 9, 2017. This is a president that is serious about protecting our law enforcement personnel.

Executive Order 13775 Providing an Order of Succession within the Department of Justice. This order specifically reverses changes made to the DOJ line of succession that former President Barack Obama made in executive order 13762. This was signed on February 9, 2017.

Executive Order 13776 Task Force on Crime Reduction and Public Safety. This was signed on February 9, 2017. This was put in place to reduce crime in America and restore public safety in our communities. Focusing on the high rate of violent crime and developing policies that address our illegal immigration and drug trafficking.

Executive Order 13777 Regulatory Reform Agenda. This was signed on February 24,2017. It is the policy of the United States to alleviate unnecessary regulatory burdens placed on the American people.

Executive Order 13778 Restoring the Rule of Law, Federalism, and Economic Growth by Reviewing the "Waters of the United States" Rule. It is in the national interest to ensure that the Nation's navigable waters are kept free from pollution, while at the same time promoting economic growth, minimizing regulatory uncertainty, and showing due regard for the roles of the Congress and the States under the Constitution. This was signed on February 28, 2017.

Executive Order 13779 The White House Initiative to Promote Excellence and Innovation at Historically Black Colleges and Universities. Historically Black colleges and universities have made extraordinary contributions. For more than 150 years, produced many of our Nation's leaders in business, government, academia, and the military, and have helped create a black middle class. These institutions are important engines of economic growth and public service, and they are proven ladders of intergenerational advancement.

Executive Order 13780 Protecting the Nation from Foreign Terrorist Entry into the United States. This was signed on March 6, 2017. This places limits on travel to the U.S. from certain countries, and by all refugees who do not possess either a visa or valid travel documents. According to its terms on March 16, 2017, this executive order revoked and replaced Executive Order 13769 issued January 27, 2017.

Executive Order 13781 Comprehensive Plan for Reorganizing the Executive Branch. This was signed on March 13, 2017. This order is intended to improve the efficiency, effectiveness, and accountability of the executive branch by directing the Director of the Office of Management and Budget (Director) to propose a plan to reorganize governmental functions and eliminate unnecessary agencies.

Getting rid of more governmental control should be seen as good.

Executive Order 13782 Revocation of Federal Contracting Executive Orders. This was signed on March 27, 2017. This Executive order revokes three prior Executive Orders by former President Obama, Executive Order 13673, which was to promote economy and efficiency in procurement by contracting with responsible sources who comply with labor laws. Executive Order 13683 covers prescribe the following regulations governing the preparation, presentation, filing, and publication of Executive orders and proclamations. This was to amend Executive Order 11030, which was signed June 19, 1962. The last one was Executive Order 13738. This order was to promote economy and efficiency in procurement by contracting with responsible sources who comply with labor laws.

Executive Order 13783 Promoting Energy Independence and Economic Growth. This was signed on March 28, 2017. to promote a clean and safe development of our Nation's vast energy resources, while at the same time avoiding regulatory burdens that unnecessarily encumber energy production, constrain economic growth, and prevent job creation. With just 60 days into office the President is working feverishly to make America great. Let's not forget he is not a politician, but rather a businessman, and he is getting down to business.

Executive Order 13784 Establishing the President's Commission on Combating Drug Addiction and the Opioid Crisis. This was signed on March 29, 2017. This was to combat the scourge of drug abuse, addiction, and overdose (drug addiction), including opioid abuse and addiction.

Executive Order 13785 Establishing the Enhanced Collection and Enforcement of Antidumping and Countervailing Duties and Violations of Trade and Customs Laws. This was signed on March 31, 2017. Importers that unlawfully evade antidumping and countervailing duties expose United States employers to unfair competition and deprive the Federal Government of lawful revenue. As of May 2015, $2.3 billion in antidumping and countervailing duties owed to the Government remained uncollected.

Executive Order 13786 Regarding the Omnibus Report on Significant Trade Deficits. This was signed on March 31, 2017. This is to promote commerce by strengthening our relationships with our trading partners, vigorously enforcing our Nation's trade laws, improving the overall conditions for competition and trade, and ensuring the strength of our manufacturing and defense industrial bases.

Executive Order 13787 Providing an Order of Succession Within the Department of Justice. This was signed on March 31, 2017. This revoked Executive Order 13775, while establishing new directives.

Executive Order 13788 Buy American and Hire American. This was signed on April 18, 2017. Buy American Laws" means all statutes, regulations, rules, and Executive Orders relating to Federal procurement or Federal grants including those that refer to "Buy America" or "Buy American" that require, or provide a preference for, the purchase or acquisition of goods, products, or materials produced in the United States, including iron, steel, and manufactured goods.

This was one of those Executive Orders that helped get him elected. He shouted loud and proudly that America should come first. He is listening to the American people and representing us with confidence.

Executive Order 13789 Identifying and Reducing Tax Regulatory Burdens. This was signed on April 21, 2017. The Federal tax system should be simple, fair, efficient, and pro-growth. The purposes of tax regulations should be to bring clarity to the already complex Internal Revenue Code.

The Executive Orders that are being implemented are being done for the good of our nation, with common sense being put ahead of the political correctness virus.

Executive Order 13790 Promoting Agriculture and Rural Prosperity in America. to promote American agriculture and protect the rural communities where food, fiber, forestry, and many of our renewable fuels are cultivated. This was signed on April 25, 2017.

Executive Order 13791 Enforcing Statutory Prohibitions on Federal Control of Education. This was signed on April 26, 2017, to restore the proper division of power under the Constitution between the Federal Government and the States and to further the goals of, and to ensure strict compliance with, statutes that prohibit Federal interference with State and local control over education. This Executive Order covers Common Core.

Executive Order 13792 Review of Designations under the Antiquities Act. This was signed on April 26, 2017. The United States Secretary of Interior shall conduct a review of all Presidential designations or expansions of designations under the Antiquities Act made since January 1, 1996, where the designation covers more than 100,000 acres, where the designation after expansion covers more than 100,000 acres, or where the Secretary determines that the designation or expansion was made without adequate public outreach and coordination with relevant stakeholders, to determine whether each designation or expansion conforms to the policy.

As we continue on know that this information on the Executive Orders came from Wikipedia.

Executive Order 13793 Improving Accountability and Whistleblower at the Department of Veterans Affairs. This was signed on April 27, 2017. This order is intended to improve accountability and whistleblower protection at the Department of Veterans Affairs (VA) by directing the Secretary of Veterans Affairs (Secretary) to establish within the VA an Office of Accountability and Whistleblower Protection and to appoint a Special Assistant to serve as Executive Director of the Office.

Executive Order 13794 Establishment of the American Technology Council. This order was signed on April 28,2017. It is the policy of the United States to promote the secure, efficient, and economical use of information technology to achieve its missions. Americans deserve better digital services from their Government.

Executive Order 13795 Implementing an America-First Offshore Energy Strategy. This was signed on April 28, 2017. America must put the energy needs of American families and businesses first and continue implementing a plan that ensures energy security and economic vitality for decades to come.

We will cover two more Executive Orders for the month of April, making 33 Executive Orders in just four months. While these may only appear, to be official documents, know that these documents make sense. Know they make America, better for all.

Executive Order 13796 Addressing Trade Agreement Violations and Abuses. This was signed on April 29, 2017. Every trade agreement and investment agreement entered into by the United States, and all trade relations and trade preference programs of the United States, should enhance our economic growth, contribute favorably to our balance of trade, and strengthen the American manufacturing base.

Executive Order 13797 Establishment of the Office of Trade and Manufacturing Policy. This was signed April 29, 2017. The mission of the OTMP is to defend and serve American workers and domestic manufacturers while advising the President on policies to increase economic growth, decrease the trade deficit, and strengthen the United States manufacturing and defense industrial bases.

Executive Order 13798 Promoting Free Speech and Religious Liberty. This was signed on May 4, 2017, to guide the executive branch in formulating and implementing policies with implications for the religious liberty of persons and organizations in America, and to further compliance with the Constitution and with applicable statutes and Presidential Directives.

Executive Order 13799 Establishment of the Presidential Advisory Commission on Election Integrity. This is in order to promote fair and honest Federal elections.

Executive Order 13800 Strengthening the Cyber Security of Federal Networks and Critical Infrastructure. This was signed on May 11, 2017. Its IT and data should be secured responsibly using all United States Government capabilities. The President will hold heads of executive departments and agencies (agency heads) accountable for managing cybersecurity risk to their enterprises.

Executive Order 13801 Expanding Apprenticeship in America. This was signed on June 15, 2017. America's education systems and workforce development programs are in need of reform. Many colleges and universities fail the students, often graduating them without the needed skills necessary to obtain a high-paying job, while placing them further in debt.

Executive Order 13802 Amendment of Executive Order 13597. This was signed on June 21, 2017. Executive Order 13597 Establishing Visa and Foreign Visitor Processing Goals and the Task Force on Travel and Competitiveness. It was signed January 19, 2012 by President Barack Obama.

Executive Order 13803 Revival of the National Space Council. This was signed on June 30, 2017. The National Space Council (Council) was established by Title V of Public Law 100-685 and Executive Order 12675 of April 20, 1989 (Establishing the National Space Council). The Council was tasked with advising and assisting the President regarding national space policy and strategy.

The Council was never formally disestablished, but it effectively ceased operation in 1993. This order revives the Council and provides additional details regarding its duties and responsibilities.

Executive Order 13804 Amendment of Executive Order 13761. This was signed on July 11, 2017. The order changes the date by which the Secretary of State, in consultation with the Secretary of the Treasury, the Director of National Intelligence, and the Administrator of the U.S. Agency for International Development, is to provide a report to the President on the Government of Sudan's progress. There is more information regarding notifying the president.

Executive Order 13805 Establishing a Presidential Advisory Council on Infrastructure. This was signed on July 19, 2017. to advance infrastructure projects that create high-quality jobs for American workers, enhance productivity, improve quality of life, protect the environment, and strengthen economic growth.

So far all Executive Orders appear to be making America great again. These orders are being executed not by a politician, but a businessman who is using commonsense and good business decisions. President Trump continues to accomplish the goals he stated he would when he was running his campaign for president.

America First

Executive Order 13806 Assessing and Strengthening the Manufacturing and Defense Industrial Base and Supply Chain Resiliency of the United States. This was signed on July 21, 2017. The ability of the United States to maintain readiness, and to surge in response to an emergency, directly relates to the capacity, capabilities, and resiliency of our manufacturing and defense industrial base and supply chains.

Executive Order 13807 Establishing Discipline and Accountability in the Environmental Review and Permitting Process for Infrastructure Projects. This was signed August 15,2017. America needs increased infrastructure investment to strengthen our economy, enhance our competitiveness in world trade, create jobs and increase wages for our workers, and reduce the costs of goods and services for our families.

Executive Order 13808 Imposing Sanctions with Respect to the Situation in Venezuela. This was signed on August 25,2017. The Executive Order prohibits transactions related to provision of financing for, and other dealings in (i) new debt of Petroleos de Venezuela, S.A.

Executive Order 13809 Restoring State, Tribal and Local Law Enforcement's access to Life Saving Equipment and Resources. Executive Order 13688 of January 16, 2015 (Federal Support for Local Law Enforcement Equipment Acquisition), is hereby revoked. This was signed on August 28, 2017.

Executive Order 13810 Imposing Additional Sanctions With Respect to North Korea. This was signed on September 20, 2017. This was due to the total disregard of other countries safety and ours, by North Korea continuing to launch nuclear missile tests.

Executive Order 13811 Continuance of Certain Federal Advisory Committees. This was signed on September 29, 2017. This covers over 32 different committees, ranging in so many groups that naming them may be overwhelming.

Executive Order 13812 Revocation of Executive Order Creating Labor-Management Forums. This was signed on September 29, 2017. Public expenditures on the Council and related forums have produced few benefits to the public, and they should, therefore, be discontinued.

Executive Order 13813 Promoting Healthcare Choice and Competition Across the United States. to facilitate the purchase of insurance across State lines and the development and operation of a healthcare system that provides high-quality care at affordable prices for the American people. This is to correct the Patient Protection and Affordable Care Act. This was signed October 12, 2017.

Executive Order 13814 Amending Executive Order 13223. This was signed on October 20, 2017. Ordering the Ready Reserve of the Armed Forces to Active Duty and Delegating Certain Authorities to the Secretary of Defense and the Secretary of Transportation.

Executive Order 13815 Resuming the United States Refugee Admissions Program with Enhanced Vetting Capabilities. This was signed on October 24, 2017, to protect its people from terrorist attacks and other public-safety threats. Screening and vetting procedures associated with determining which foreign nationals may enter the United States.

Executive Order 13816 Revising the Seal for the National Credit Union Administration. This was signed on December 8, 2017. The National Credit Union Administration Board has caused to be made, and has recommended approval of, a new seal of office for the National Credit Union Administration.

Executive Order 13817 A Federal Strategy To Ensure Secure and Reliable Supplies of Critical Minerals. This was signed on December 20, 2017. The United States is heavily reliant on imports of certain mineral commodities that are vital to the Nation's security and economic prosperity.

Executive Order 13818 Blocking the Property of Persons Involved in Serious Human Rights Abuse or Corruption. This was signed on December 21, 2017. The United States seeks to impose tangible and significant consequences on those who commit serious human rights abuse or engage in corruption.

Executive Order 13819 Adjustments of Certain Rates of Pay. The rates of basic pay or salaries for the following offices and positions, Vice President, and Congress. This was signed on December 22, 2017. This was his last Executive Order for 2017.

When Donald Trump ran for President, he let everyone know what he was for and against. He dove right in, taking on Obama Care which was doomed right from the start. He stated he would address Isis and terrorist activity. At the moment Isis appears to have diminished immensely. He has taken on infrastructure, and sanctuary cities Establishing ethics in Washington D.C., and much, much more. He stated he was going to drain the swamp. Looking at some key players, we'll see he is working on this. We will go in to his first ten Executive Orders of 2018. Here we will finish off on this part of his accomplishments.

Executive Order 13820 Termination of Executive Order 13799 (Presidential Advisory Commission on Election Integrity). This was signed on January 3, 2018. Executive Order 13799, is hereby revoked, and the Presidential Advisory Commission on Election Integrity is accordingly terminated.

Executive Order 13821 Streamlining and Expediting Requests to Locate Broadband Facilities in Rural America. This was signed on January 8, 2018. Americans need access to reliable, affordable broadband internet service to succeed in today's information-driven, global economy.

Executive Order 13822 Supporting Our Veterans During Their Transition From Uniformed Service to Civilian Life. This was signed on January 9, 2018. It is the policy of the United States to support the health and well-being of uniformed service members and veterans.

Executive Order 13823 Protecting America Through Lawful Detention of Terrorists. This was signed on January 30, 2018.

Executive Order 13824 President's Council on Sports, Fitness, and Nutrition. This was signed on February 26, 2018.

Executive Order 13825 2018 Amendments to the Manual for Courts-Martial, United States. This was signed on March 1, 2018.

Executive Order 13826 Federal Interagency Council on Crime Prevention and Improving Reentry. This was signed on March 7, 2018.

Executive Order 13827 Taking Additional Steps to Address the Situation in Venezuela. This was signed on March 19, 2018.

Executive Order 13828 Reducing Poverty in America by Promoting Opportunity and Economic Mobility. This was signed April 10, 2018.

Executive Order 13829 Task Force on the United States Postal System. This was signed on April 12, 2018.

Currently the President is working on border security and the DACA crisis, along with many other unseen matters. The President is doing a good job, those that elected him are happy with his persistence and his unwavering commitment to making America great again. As we view whether there is, or isn't resistance.

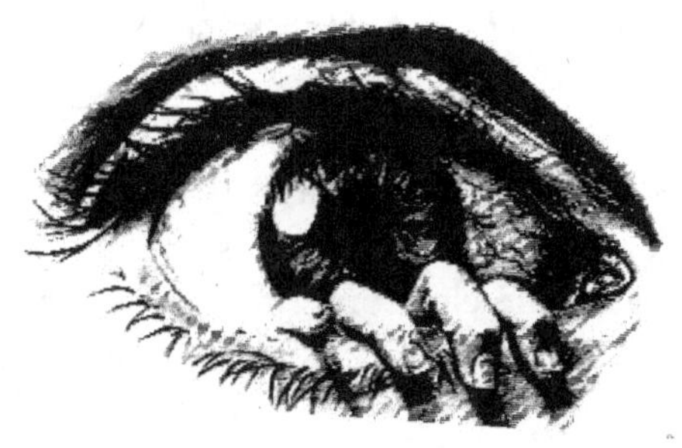

RESISTANCE
RIGHTING THE WRONG

This chapter is about addressing and exposing those that wish only to resist the President of the United States. Those that seek to destroy, infect, or harm the President's character for the purpose of eliminating his ability to do his job. They focus only on their own agenda, showing no remorse for the character assassination of our newly elected president. Donald Trump came in to the arena an outsider. He was laughed at in the beginning as they didn't take him serious. He came into the Presidential candidacy an underdog and single-handedly took out nine candidates, leaving him as the Republican Contender.

I grew up believing that the news was strictly events that were being recorded and reported for the purpose of informing the viewers of current events that were happening live. The truth is, these events that we see on television are often edited, rehearsed, or just misleading.

If we start with the first Republican debate, we see the first question asked. Can I see a show of hands from those unwilling to pledge support to the eventual nominee of the Republican Party? Donald Trump stood alone as he said he was unwilling to commit to that request.

They tried to make him look as though he were not a true Republican, and that he was just trying to help Hillary Clinton in the election. Once he became the Republican leader, others of his party turned their back and refused to support him while on stage that night publicly lied knowing they would resist and said nothing.

Senator Rand Paul states, "That's what's wrong, he buys and sells politicians of all stripes." The truth is Donald Trump is not your typical politician. He is a businessman who has to claim the political title of a president to accomplish making America great again.

Do you think there was a coincidence when Megan Kelly was chosen as a commentator in the Republican debate? Is it possible she was chosen to ask questions that might make Donald Trump respond harshly, making him appear as a bully picking on an innocent female? As we continue keep an open mind and put America first.

The next question that was asked to Donald Trump was the following. "Mr. Trump one of the things people love about you, is you speak your mind and you don't use a politicians filter, however that is not without its downside, in particular when it comes to women. You've called women you don't like fat pigs, dogs, slobs, and disgusting animals. Your twitter account."

Donald Trump interrupts, "Only Rosie O'Donnell." Donald smiles as he lets her finish.

"No, it wasn't your twitter account, for the record it was well beyond Rosie O'Donnell." Megan Kelly continued as she stated "you had several disparaging comments about women's looks. You once told a contestant on Celebrity Apprentice, it would be a pretty picture to see her on her knees. Does that sound like a temperament of a man we should elect as president?"

He replies "I think the big problem we have is being politically correct."

Donald Trump's character was attacked from the beginning in a carefully orchestrated manner. They tried making him look like a spoiled rich bully who lacked a restraint to communicate in a society designed for just a select few. They tried to present him as spontaneous, volatile, and unpredictable, way too dangerous for the office of president.

As we start with the news media attacking his Executive Order 13769. They try to portray this order as a Muslim ban when it was specifically targeting 7 countries known to house terrorist.

The Trump administration instituted a pause on the admission of foreign nationals coming from those countries for 90 days and halted the refugee programs from all countries for 120 days to beef up the vetting process. These are within his powers. There were other Muslim countries, approximately 40 other countries where they still were allowed to continue as usual. The media promoted this to the American people as a Muslim ban.

CNN reported that they tied with Fox News on ratings on Inauguration Day. Supposedly the ratings weren't even close. In their defense, most companies are going to lie to make their ratings look better. CNN is not alone when talking ratings.

Time News was caught in a lie on reporting on an Executive Order, then stated it was due to President Trump. This was reported by Ryan Teague Beckwith. Time News never did apologize.

Washington Post "Fact Checker" Attempts to Gin Up Dissent Against Trump. Glenn Kessler, supposedly used his twitter feed to manufacture fake news against Trump. He called on foreign-service officers to sign a dissent memo, which would then become an anti-Trump story.

The media's lack of reporting on foreign born terrorists. Between 2001 and 2014, 380 foreign-born terrorists were convicted in America, 40 of those were refugees. Failure to report the news is the same as lying. It is being deceptive with its audience.

According to the FBI, dozens of bomb making terrorists that are believed to have attacked American troops over in Iraq and Afghanistan, may have been mistakenly allowed access in to the United States as war refugees.

The Associated Press reported that Donald Trump's voter fraud expert was registered in three different states during 2016. They reported this in a manner as to make it look like Trump's expert was deceitful as well. The problem is, his registration was only active in one state. In an election year if you are not sure where your place of residence will be, then it just makes sense to cover your bases, especially on matters involving our country, and our safety.

The media reported that Dick Cheney condemned President Trump's executive order that was signed on Friday. The truth was that he condemned Trump's proposed Muslim Ban in December 2015 and not the executive order that had been thoroughly thought through.

The Media reported that the Refugee pause was based on countries that Donald Trump's own companies did not do business with. Seven nations that fall in under the Executive Order don't include countries with Trump Organization Projects. They forget to mention that they probably wouldn't want to do business in any of those seven countries either. The media are a master manipulator when it comes to deceiving the people while portraying themselves as righteous.

ABC News accuses Donald Trump of not having a family picture in the Oval Office. This is based supposedly off just one photograph. They also forget to mention he had hardly stepped in to the White House. I am sure a family picture is not a priority when it comes to just taking office, and he is having to fight with those in his own administration who have been trying to sabotage from within. If he did have any family pictures, they would then say he was egotistic, arrogant, and self-centered. It just comes down to the media focusing only on what it can spin for its own agenda. Terry Moran is the Chief Correspondent of ABC News. Someone of this statue is going to focus on family pictures. To me this is beyond a petty and ridiculous.

The media, and those on the left have tried to portray President Trump as part of ISIS recruitment tool. They try to present the president of being too tough when it comes to the Muslim ban, and this has caused the Muslim world of joining ISIS. I think ISIS has been neutralized and is starting to diminish. We hardly hear anything about them anymore. Why is that? What is the reason the media has stopped talking about them for? Could it be they are being dealt with successfully?

Another example is a tweet that included the title Muslim ban, Politico's Blake Hounshell and CNN's Jake Tapper, reported on a tweet from Mike Flynn Jr., son of Trump's National Security Advisor, stating he had declared Trump's refugee pause a "Muslim Ban." If these seven countries were banned due to their radical beliefs and support of terrorists, why does the media not address this? Why do they try to smear the reason, with the word Muslim?

The Washington Post's Josh Rogin supposedly spread a lie that there was a "mass exodus of senior Foreign Service officers" at the State Department. All of it due to Trump. The truth is the White House asked for resignations, which are standard procedure.

The Washington Post reported on January 25, 2017 that "The State Department's entire senior administrative team just resigned." Other headlines appeared like the following examples.

SALON: **Mutiny at Foggy Bottom: State Department management resigns in masse**

THE ROOT: **State Department Senior Management Team Resigns Instead of Working With Trump**

JEZEBEL: **The State Department's Senior Management Just Resigned in Masse**

RAW STORY: **The 'entire senior level' of State Department management just resigned to avoid working for Trump: report.**

Maggie Haberman

✔ @maggieNYT

Other than San Bernardino shootings, has there been a terrorist attack involving a non-US-born attacker since 9/11?

Maggie Haberman is a White House Correspondents for New York Times. She, should think before speaking. There were the Boston Marathon bombers, The Beltway Snipers, Fort Hood Shooting, Ohio State University attack, and many more. Just go back to the chapter America's borders, building the wall. To be a great reporter or writer, you must know the subject. Don't let your own opinions get included in your report. How many stories get reported but thrown on the back page or written in a manner that get lost between the pages.

The media reported that President Obama did not discriminate against Christian Refugees when the numbers show different. The numbers report The United States has accepted 10,801 Syrian refugees, of whom 56 are Christian. Not 56 percent; 56 total, out of 10,801. The BBC says that 10 percent of all Syrians are Christian, which would mean 2.2 million Christians. It looks like we are short on the Christian Refugees that we are allowed.

This data gets unreported for some reason. It appears these deceptive practices are the reason we have to deal with our borders now. America is becoming a place where terror occurs from within our borders. Where civilians are targeted like innocent lambs. We know that President Obama was soft on holding others accountable for their actions, except for Americans, Christians, or White males. How many times did we see Obama speak with no American flag present? President Trump is all about America, and Americans. The media have targeted him from the beginning as most these were reported in his first couple weeks. As we now move on to the resistance from our Hollywood stars.

Lady Gaga was asked if she was a Trump fan, she laughed. This is a singer who hides her face from the very people that go to watch her perform and pay her salary.

Matt Damon commented about Donald Trump's first GOP debate, where he talked about deporting 11 million immigrants, and building a 1,900 mile wall to prevent further immigration into the country. Matt presented these actions as though if you live South of the border you are seen as inhuman. He also stated you are also talking about my wife and daughters. The truth is Donald Trump was talking only about the illegal ones, so if Matt Damon's wife and daughters are not illegal immigrants he was not talking about them.

In regard To Matt Damon's view on gun control, he believes we Americans should not have guns. He forgets though that in his movies where he has made millions of dollars from us watching his movies. He uses guns to portray himself as a badass. Is he willing to return all the money he made from the movies that have guns in them?

Madonna is and was an awesome singer yet her words about the president and the White House command accountability. Madonna stated "It took us this horrific moment of darkness to wake us the fuck up. It seems we have all slipped into a false sense of comfort that justice will prevail and that good would win in the end. Well good did not win this election, but good will end in the end. There is power in our unity, and that no opposing force stands a chance in the face of true solidarity. To our detractors that insist that this march will not add up to anything, fuck you."

"Yes I am angry. Yes I am outraged.   Yes I have thought an awful lot about blowing up the White House."

Once again we have a celebrity who is liked by millions threatening the president's home, where he works, sleeps, and entertains. What would happen if someone said they thought about blowing up one of the stages she was on during a concert? Her comments were made during the Women's march.

CNN was quick to come in and attempt to save the celebrities words, saying they were taken out of context. CNN is not a supporter of President Trump. They are the biggest advocate of Hillary Clinton. There is no confusion in her meaning. The words came straight out of her mouth.

Kathy Griffin was once known as a comedian, but has since been viewed as a celebrity that has gone over the edge. She used a prop that not only disrespects our president but  encouraged violence using ISIS methods. This picture could be used by Isis making it look like we Americans want what they do. This was a threat against our president. She should have had to do time. I would like to see her standing holding that head in front of the troops in Iraq and see how she explains herself.

Chris Wallace commented during a debate between then Presidential candidates, Donald Trump, and Hillary Clinton. He stated, "There is a tradition in this country, is the peaceful transition of power. No matter how hard fought a campaign is that at the end of the campaign the looser succeeds to the winner. Not saying you are necessarily going to be the looser, or the winner, but the looser concedes to the winner and that the country comes together, in part for the good of the country." He asks whether Donald Trump would commit.

They honestly believed he would lose. Now that Trump is President those that pleaded with him to succeed, are now pushing to resist. They are putting their party before their country. The corrupt media's bias only shows the American people the truth in which the media spins events for their cause.

Celebrities are used often times to sway the voters their way. They believe that they are loved so much that it does not matter what they say, just trust them.

Let us look at some of their comments during the Emmy.

"We know that the biggest star of last year was Donald Trump. We all know the Emmys mean a lot to Donald Trump. He was nominated multiple times for Celebrity Apprentice, but he never won. I'll tell you what. If he had won an Emmy, he wouldn't have run for president. The president has complained repeatedly that the Emmys are rigged. He tweeted that Seth Meyers is hosting the Emmy awards is a total joke. He is very awkward with almost no talent. Marbles in his mouth."

As they zoom the camera towards the stars seated in the audience. Seth opens his mouth letting marbles fall out. This was staged and planned. They were clearly trying to politicize the Emmys. They mentioned unlike the presidency the Emmy goes to the popular vote. They are trying to speak out about Hillary Clinton losing when she was said to have the majority of votes.

They bring out special guest American political strategist and former White House Press Secretary and Communications Director for President Donald Trump. Sean Spicer. As he wheels out a presidential podium. Was he there for ratings? Was he there due to being disgruntle? Maybe he wanted more exposer for himself. The Emmy Award is an American award that recognizes excellence in the television industry, and is the equivalent of an Academy Award for film, the Tony Award for theater, and a Grammy Award for music.

None of these awards mention attacking and disrespecting our president, yet many of them do. One of the Black actors gets up on stage and says he wants to thank President Trump for making Blacks, number one on the most oppressed list. Another actress said "We have a great final season we are about to start filming, with a lot of surprises that our writers have cooked up. We did have a whole story line about impeachment, but we abandoned that because we were worried someone else might get to it first.

Alec Baldwin was on the Jimmy Kimmel show and while we all know it is about making people laugh, they were pushing insults attacking President Trump's intelligence.

They were using his difficulty of word selection as though he were stupid. Do you see them talk about Hillary Clinton that way? What about Nancy Pelosi, Maxine Waters? We will get to these people later. Donald Trump has been very successful throughout his life. He did beat all the Republican candidates, and the Democrat's own, Hillary Clinton. I have no problem with comedians making fun of others, that is what they do, but when they carefully target, orchestrate, and apply these in a manner to insight others for their own cause I think it is wrong. When celebrities talk about change through intimidation, threats, force, or just blowing up the White House, they should be held accountable for their words and gestures.

We must remember how they say it, is just as important, as what they are saying. Great leaders lead by example. They have to listen. They may not agree, but at least they will hear the other sides point of view. I am addressing this, because the next group we're going to be discussing are the politicians. The politicians are known often as lawyers, the elite, and two faced. I am not saying they all are, just that they are many times seen in these views by the rest of society. They are above the law, better than the average Joe. The Democrats currently are seen as the party of Resistance.

If we go back to the beginning, we can view Hillary Clinton's down fall. We can view her character, along with unrealistic views of why she never became president. She wanted to blame FBI Director James Comey's letter, based on a false memo from the Russians.

Hillary Clinton refused to look at her E-mail scandal, where she sent and received E-mails through an unsecure company. She risked highly classified materials knowingly. She attempted to ignore the policies that were put in place for the purpose of safety and security of our country. She viewed the country's documents as her own. She failed to accept responsibility for her own actions.

Hillary brought up sexism as she tries to present herself as more a woman than a presidential candidate. She tries presenting Donald Trump as a male chauvinist pig, a bully, and a white aggressive male. She probably thought the female card would work for her, like the Black card worked for Obama.

Hillary brought up the electoral system. She just made sure she knew whether it was going to help or hurt her before she used this card. She blamed Wikileaks on the constant dripping of information over weeks. Hillary Clinton blamed the Right-Wing media, along with Mainstream Media. Many made their minds up earlier. When she was being questioned on Benghazi, and she stated "The fact is we have four dead Americans," was it because of a protest, or was it because guys out for a walk one night decided to go kill some American? What difference at this point does it make?"

To those that have served their country, putting on a uniform and willing to sacrifice your life for your country, it makes all the difference in the world. Hillary has always portrayed herself as a victim, rather than the one who should be held accountable for her actions, or lack thereof.

She talked about having to inject money into the Democratic National Convention. Was this money that came out of the Clinton Foundation?

While she ran for president, I did not hear any views on what she wanted to do to make America better. She only screamed resist, defy, protest.

Hillary mentioned the 1,000 Russian agents that assisted in delivering those earlier messages. She mentioned Vladimir Putin wanted her to fail and went out of his way to help Donald Trump with the election. She also mentioned citizens uniting against her in away to prevent her from becoming president. Now this, I believe. It was those that united against her she called deplorable. She is forgetting one thing. We the American people do the voting. We elected a president that hadn't yet made wrong decisions in the White House, or thrived in Washington living off wealth of the people.

The definition of Deplorable means strong condemnation. This just goes to show you that anyone that disagrees with her is seen in this category. Ask her secret service agents how she saw them. Some say she looked down on them, viewing them as peasants. Do I know this for a fact? No, only have read articles about this at different times and through different papers and media resources. We must not forget she has a lot of political pull. She has yet to have been touched, or held accountable for her E-mail scandal. Only time will tell. meanwhile she will bounce in and out of the media to inject her resistance on our new president, who we voted in.

Nancy Pelosi is another key figure. She is an American politician, currently serving as the Minority Leader of the United States House of Representatives.

Let's view some of her comments.

"This takes preparation, this takes knowledge, this takes judgment, and clearly it takes preparation, which the President didn't make. Clearly he didn't know what he was getting into, and now he is walking away from it." This was about the North Korea summit. In the end President Trump did get somewhere with North Korea.

Nancy Pelosi spoke to a crowd of dreamers on one occasion and when she stated, "for a long time we have been fighting the fight for the dreamers." The crowd boos her and starts yelling and screaming back at her. She loses her composer as they call her a liar. She gets in an argument with the very people she is there trying to represent.

Some Democrats are distancing themselves from Nancy Pelosi's comment, on calling tax breaks crumbs. Rep, Keith Ellison (D-Mn) stated that if you could pick up $1,000.00 or $900.00 it could help. The problem with Nancy Pelosi, is that she accordingly to Chain E-mail will make $803,700.00 a year for life. This means the $1000.00, or $900.00 really is bread crumbs, when you compare it to her world, and the rest of Washington. According to investmentwatchblog.com Nancy Pelosi has a $196 million net worth on $193,000 Senators salary. These are rich and wealthy people that run our country and have lost the reality of the value of the dollar to the working-class people.

Is President Trump rich? Yes he is, but he is also not receiving a salary. He has donated his first quarter 2018 salary to the Department of Veterans Affairs. His second quarter he donated to the Department of Education. Name me one other president that has ever done this. President Trump is rich, but sometimes you have to fight rich with rich. Meaning he can't be bought when it comes to the welfare of our country.

Nancy Pelosi stated, "This is like Armageddon, in terms of bonuses Americans receive vs crumbs that they are giving to workers to put the snooze on, is so pathetic. This is like giving you a bowl of doggy doo and put a cherry on top and call it a Chocolate Sunday." She also had commented, "May's jobs report shows that strong employment numbers, mean little to the families hit with soaring new costs under the Republican's watch."

Nancy Pelosi unfortunately is out of touch with middle America., who are getting bonuses and pay raises, who now have left the unemployment market and are now working. The unemployment is the lowest it has been especially for minorities.

Nancy stated, "Hip Hip hooray unemployment is down. What does that mean to my life? I need a bigger paycheck. This isn't just about the unemployment rate. It is about wages rising in our country so that consumer confidence is restored. Because our economy will never fully reach its possibilities unless we increase the consumers' confidence." The consumer confidence is at its highest. I guess if you do not like what the statistics show you just say what you want and hope no one will fact check you.

The last thing Democrats want is for minorities to benefit under the Republican party, so they try focusing on anything that will distract them from the truth of accomplishment. If they lose the minorities, then the Democrats will have no one to rally for them.

Maxine Waters is an American politician. She is serving as the U.S. Representative for California's 43rd Congressional District since 2013. She had previously served in the 35th and 29th Districts. Maxine Waters is a member and former chair of the Congressional Black Caucus.

Maxine Waters is another high ranking key member of the Democratic party. She commented at one of her rallies saying the following. "If you see anybody from that cabinet in a restaurant, in a department store, at a gasoline station, you get out and create a crowd, and you push back on them, and you tell them you're not welcomed."

She is encouraging violence by pushing others to resist against the Trump cabinet members. She wanted them to invade the cabinet member's personal space and threaten their family and places where they go to relax and do business. What happened with being a professional, civil, and respectful?

On MSNBC she again stated, "They are going to protest them, they are going to absolutely harass them until they tell the president, no I can't hang with you." This should be addressed as a hate crime. Harassing others because of who they hang with. They do not address a topic of concern, but identify Trump cabinet members to harass, intimidate, and resist.

On the MSNBC show Maxine Waters was standing next to Congressmen Engel who the MSNBC commentator was speaking too. As he was asked a question, he is interrupted by Maxine Waters who thinks they were talking to her. It just presents herself as not very attentive.

She presents herself as less than knowledgeable when she commented on Trump wrapping his arms around Vladimir Putin while Putin is continuing to advance into Korea. She stated she was a millennial once, but no longer. I think she misunderstands the term millennial.

Sarah Huckabee, the White House Press Secretary was denied service and asked to leave at the Red Hen restaurant in Virginia. Does this not scream follow through, "You're Not Welcomed?" This is what Maxine Waters is about. On the controversial television show The View, Sunny Hostin, a commentator said she was not forced to leave, she was asked to leave. Really? Is this not harassment? Let me think about this a second. I am sitting waiting to order a meal. I get asked to leave if I do not leave how do you think my food will get prepared and served to me? That is like making your wife who knows your about to divorce her fix you one more meal.

This is why Sunny Hostin was on the View and not serving the community, or her country. Sunny joined the View in season 20 as a senior legal correspondent and analyst. In February 2016. Before that, was a host and legal analyst at CNN. I would not be searching her out for legal advice unless you're prepared to do time.

Maxine Waters states she wants peaceful protests, when she is by herself, but in front of a crowd she wants loud, forceful resistance. She wants those that are against her to pay. What type of crowd do you think will follow her? It will be a crowd much like Ferguson, Missouri, or Black Lives Matter organization.

Let us look at Elizabeth Warren

Elizabeth Warren is an American politician. She has served as a U.S. Senator from Massachusetts, since January 3, 2013, and Vice Chair of the Senate Democratic Caucus, since January 3, 2017. She was previously Chair of the Congressional Oversight Panel, from November 25, 2008 to November 15, 2010, and Special Advisor for the Consumer Financial Protection Bureau, from September 17, 2010 to August 1, 2011.

Elizabeth has verified English, with smaller amounts (to varying degrees) of English, Cornish, Swiss-German, Scottish, Welsh, Irish, Scots-Irish/Northern Irish, and Swedish, ancestry. She has stated that she was told by her family, that one of her maternal great-great-great-grandmothers, Neoma Sarah Smith (popularly known as O.C. Sarah Smith), was of Cherokee Native American background.

Did Elizabeth Warren put this on her resume to help her political career? This isn't the first time someone used their race for power, or to get ahead. She commented on President Donald Trump's first 90 days, while on the television show (The Political View).

One of the commentators comments on Trump being in there for 90 days. Elizabeth then replies, "it is like dog years or something." To me this is unprofessional that a Senator responds about the President of the United States in this manner. Elizabeth Warren was asked what has he done right so far? She responds, "I take that question very seriously. I fought very hard to get Hillary Clinton in to office. I did not want to see Donald Trump as president. He promised he was going to be for working people. It's not the way he says, or his tweets, I just keep watching what he is actually doing. He signed off on a law that makes it easier for employers to steal their employee's wages. He signed off on a law that makes it easier for companies that kill, or maim their employees to keep it hidden. He signed off on a law that makes it easier for investment advisors to cheat pensioners and retirees. Knock 24 million people off their health care coverage. To raise the cost of a lot of middle-class families so that we can produce a tax cut for a handful of millionaires and billionaires." She says he is just delivering one gut punch after another. She wants to present the Obama care as successful healthcare coverage, it is not and never was.

The commentator asked her why he still has a strong following of Trump supporters? Her reply was, "Did you see the movie UP? Do you remember the dog that used to yell squirrel? Everybody would head in that direction. She states President Trump is the master of distraction. He is the master at, don't look at what I am doing, look somewhere else. She states we have to stay focused on what he does. Elizabeth stated her biggest regret is that Donald Trump is President of the United States period.

At what point will these Senators, the Minority leader, former Presidential candidate accept the President of the United States. At what point will they go back to their House of Representatives, the Senate, and White House and get back to doing business as professionals and as representatives of the people that voted for Trump?

The Democrats have spent a lot of time on television on talk shows when they should be in Washington working for you and I. They should be looking to unite our country, not divide it, as they have done through the Obama years and are attempting to still do.

Trump Supporters now have been identified as cartoon idiots that are easily misled. This just goes to show how out of touch Elizabeth Warren and the others are, when it comes to our financial stability, border security, and making America great again.

The name of this movie might be "UP", but it is us deplorable Americans, and now identified as cartoon idiots labeled by Elizabeth Warren that are fed up. We are tired of the Mockery, lunacy, and deceptive practices of the Democratic Party, that only wishes to resist.

RELIGION
PERSECUTING CHRISTIANITY

Christianity, many people take for granted in the United States. While we have the freedom to choose our religion, and express ourselves through prayer, singing, preaching, and worshiping, others do not. In countries like Mexico, Colombia, Mauritania, Mali, Algeria, Azerbaijan, Oman, United Arab Emirates, and China, persecution is high to Christians. Persecution is even higher in these countries, Tunisia, Nigeria, Central African Republic, Kenya, Ethiopia, Egypt, Saudi Arabia, Turkey, Turkmenistan, Uzbekistan, and Kazakhstan. Leaving extreme persecution in Libya, Sudan, Somalia, Yemen, Iraq, Iran, Afghanistan, Pakistan, and India. To be killed because you are a Christian is wrong.

Are Americans prepared to stand against those none believers of Christ?

Those that wish to punish you because you do? One of the reasons people like to come to our country is for the freedom they receive upon entering our country. The problem now, is that we are getting those that disagree with our freedoms, especially religion and are trying to make us feel bad about being Christians.

If we look at the basic views of Christians , just in the Ten Commandments, we will see they reflect much of American's philosophy. Of course, not all will agree. but they have always done their own thing never trying to impose their beliefs on those that disagreed with them.

1. You shall have no other gods.
2. You shall not make idols.
3. You shall not misuse the name of the Lord.
4. Remember the Sabbath, keep it holy.
5. Honor your father and mother.
6. You shall not murder.
7. You shall not commit adultery.
8. You shall not steal.
9. You shall not lie.
10. You shall not covet.

We have the right to choose our religion.. Does your God have to be the same as your neighbors? Are you going to kill your neighbor because your idea of God and his idea don't match? These may sound ridiculous to you and I, as far as killing someone over these differences, but all those countries on the other page kill Christians daily for these reasons.

The second Commandment is, make no idol. How many of our politicians see themselves above the rest of us? While they try to represent us and speak on our behalf? Do they forget, or purposely try to separate church and state? While I know the commandment is talking about worshiping an idol in place of God, or in God's honor, could they see themselves as an idol to be worshiped by us? The First Amendment, was created. To protect us.

First Amendment, prohibits congress from making any law respecting an establishment of religion, impeding the free exercise of religion, abridging the freedom of speech, infringing on the freedom of the press, interfering with the right to peaceably assemble, or prohibiting the petitioning for a governmental redress of grievances.

President Trump believes in our constitution and is trying to protect it from those on the left that wish to abolish our constitution one amendment at a time.

The third commandment is not to misuse the name of the lord. I know that everyone has used the Lords name in vain at some time. I know I have. When I do I try to apologize and ask forgiveness. Christians are people that have sinned, and must repent on their sins they have committed. Christians associate decency, kindness, and fairness with Christian teachings. Love thy neighbor, do to others as you wish to have done to you.

While, we all know what we should do, many times we let our emotions dictate our response, only to regret our actions later. It is here that Christians repent, asking for forgiveness.

The 4th commandment is remembered the sabbath and keep it holy. We celebrate Sundays as the sabbath day. The Bible is the book of knowledge. It may reflect Saturday as the sabbath, but for my purpose I am just using Sunday. Our history shows American families that are Christian taking time out of their schedules on Sunday to unite the family as a whole while taking time to give thanks to the Lord. Here we use this day to teach through God's words Christian values. Be kind, respectful, courteous, help thy neighbor, and most of all love one another.

The 5th commandment is to honor your father and mother. We have been taught from an early age to respect our parents. The key to survival is learning from others that have succeeded. Our parents were once kids, students, teenagers, and young adults. They bring their knowledge and wisdom through their experiences to help their children and to pass on their good qualities to their next generation. Parents that do not, or will not teach to their children create gaps that cause bad seeds. Some that do teach still have children that become bad.

Why is it that this occurs? Who is to blame? It is not about blame; it is about faith. Pray for those that are bad and do your part to encourage them through tough times. This does not mean they should not be held accountable for their actions. We all will be held accountable for the sins we have committed when we meet the Lord.

You should not murder is the 6th commandment. Some sins will have severe consequence. We have been taught as Christians to love thy neighbor, and to respect life. Are the ones that commit murder, not Christians? Are they still able to be forgiven and given an opportunity to go to heaven? I believe they are. The Lord says vengeance is mine as in his alone. It is not for you, or I to wish vengeance on another. To do this means we do not forgive that person and therefore we should not be forgiven till we can forgive.

The 7th Commandment. You shall not commit adultery. Many view this as cheating on your spouse. To a lust at another is a sin. no matter how short. We all are guilty of this. With freedom comes great responsibility. We are tempted by lust rather than love. Love from the heart and soul. To love someone is to know them. God wants us to love him.

The 8th commandment is you shall not steal. To steal is to take from another. Taking from another, is putting yourself before them. God wants us to think of ourselves last and others first. We must sacrifice at times things we want for things we need.

The 9th commandment is to not lie. Being honest, no matter the consequences. Trust, is key here for trusting in others, is to show faith that you will be forgiven and you will accept the consequence for whatever you have done. Those that lie have not accepted their responsibility.

The 10th commandment, is not coveted. The definition means yearn, possess, or have something. To live your life through materialistic items. Our world can seem quite confusing at times, as Americans long to possess their own homes, vehicles, fame, wealth. We wish to be recognized for our accomplishments, rather than be humble, and anonymous as we have been taught through Christianity. It is through life we learn how to bring our desires of materialistic things in to perspective with our Christian values. These are the basic guidelines of Christians and how they should act. Nowhere do you hear of them condemning others for not being Christians, or wishing to kill others due to their different religious beliefs.

All we have to do is again, look at the chapter America's Borders, building the wall and see how these people that were described in this chapter harmed others due to their religious beliefs. These were not Christians, but Muslim extremists. President Trump is looking out for the American people that wish to live safely, and prosper in their own communities, and country. They should not fear those that don't like what Americans and America stands for.

Let's look at the Democrats and their views on Christianity. The Democrats stand firmly against profiling any individual on their religious beliefs. All religions should be safe from unfounded accusations. They also stand strictly against imposing any religious beliefs, or practices on those who don't necessarily support them.

Maxine Waters, stated. "If you see anybody from that cabinet in a restaurant, in a department store, at a gasoline station, you get out and create a crowd, and you push back on them, and you tell them you're not welcomed." This is not Christian behavior. They profile on those that disagree with them and then try to harass and intimidate.

Politicians are good at talking out both sides of their mouth, so at the end of their sentence your not sure who they are for. President Trump has been straight, on target, and direct. He is easy to understand.

He hasn't changed his views to appease those against him, but rather stood strong with the American people. As we continue listen to these politicians and their carefully orchestrated words.

Nancy Pelosi spoke with religious leaders on behalf of the DACA Dreamers. The preacher Reverend Jackson, said a prayer about having mercy to the dreamers, and for assistance to lead our government. He ended the prayer in Jesus name we pray, Amen. Nancy Pelosi stated, "We are proud to be with our dreamers who make America more American, with hope, determination and optimism. On their persistence on making the next generation better, those are American traits."

I think she has failed on the point that these DACA Dreamers are illegally here in our country and we Americans don't see illegal behavior as an American trait. This is the political art of painting illegal immigrants as undocumented Americans making them sound as though they are already Americans with rights. This is wrong, deceptive, and criminal.

Nancy Pelosi, said this was nothing partisan or political about defending America's dreams. Again this is not America's dreams, but illegal's dreams. Nancy Pelosi talked about the Dream Act where they wish to use border security as a hostage to negotiate, not for Americans, but the dreamers, who are here illegally, and not paying taxes. She commented on fighting for Dreamers is about respecting the values of a family, it is the heart of our faith, and identity as Americans.

It is clear that Nancy Pelosi as chosen the illegals over the citizens of America. She has done this in hopes to secure her the votes she, or her constituents may need later on.

During their rally they have Andres Ortiz who is an undocumented immigrant get up and speak. When she was 6 years old her parents migrated to the U.S. She didn't know English and stated she got bullied for not knowing the Pledge of Allegiance. Her father instilled in her the value of a better education. Why did he not instill honesty and coming to America legally? She spoke saying her brother was legal, but she was not, and that she has not been treated fairly like he has. She wasn't given the same opportunity he was. We call it being a U.S. citizen. She still graduated college with a Bachelor's Degree in business administration.

She talked about turning to God as she stated she is a person of faith. When she can't figure it out she leaves it to the Lord to figure out. She then mentions she has been directed through the Lord to speak on behalf of the dreamers. She stated she is not looking for a free pass, but compassion. Yet they nudged illegally coming into our country, breaking the law, getting an education, while preventing someone else who has been waiting patiently, and legally from entering or getting into the same college.

This is more than a free pass. What if the person that is waiting legally to enter our country dies while waiting to enter legally? They will have lost the opportunity to have fulfilled their dream to someone who came illegally.

The Democrats try presenting people in a false narrative. This rally was orchestrated carefully, in a manner to gain Christian's support and sympathy for votes. The Democrats need to build their voting numbers.

They have stood firm on the Blacks, Hispanics, college students, and are trying now to gain with the Christians. They seek out those in poverty, not to help but to enable them, driving them to become codependent on the governments assistance, which they can use to control the poverty-stricken people at a later time.

Senator Chuck Schumer of New York has basically told anyone of any religious persuasion, if you disagree with the contraception mandate in Obama care, then don't even bother starting a business. Schumer claims that religious protection is only for an individual's personal views. It does not apply to persons who own and operate a business. Now this was from 2014. His views, have no expiration date on them. He is currently the Senate Minority Leader.

President Trump has chosen Brett Michael Kavanaugh as his Supreme Court Nominee. The Democrats and those on the side of resistance have already stated before a new Supreme Court Judge would be picked they would resist. They understand the person that has been chosen is a good and fair Judge, yet they are hoping to stall to put one of their own in later on, stacking the deck on their side. They fear a conservative judge may overturn Roe vs. Wade

Roe vs. Wade. On January 22, 1973, the U.S. Supreme Court handed down its landmark decision in the case of Roe vs. Wade, which recognized that the constitutional right to privacy extends to a woman's right to make her own personal medical decisions — including the decision to have an abortion without interference from politicians.

While I am pro-life, I do feel that the government should not be able to interfere with a woman's choice on abortion, except for extenuating circumstances. There are lots of reasons women choose abortion, namely, rape, young and immature, unexpected. I feel all life is precious and should be saved. I also look at our governments many departments. The Department of Children Family Services has many times lost children through our bureaucracy. They become numbers, names, and statistics, rather than children needing assistance. It is about making money as the child become, not a member to our society, but rather a commodity to an organization that can and will prosper off the mishap of others.

I am not trying to direct this just towards the Democrats as the Republicans to try to strategize for their own agenda. What we need to know, though, is which party closest represents our needs, values, and morals? President Trump is working on draining the swamps, but it takes time. Maybe it is about finding better leadership. Leaders, looking out for the American people rather than politicians who use Washington as a harbor. President Trump has made lots of decisions so far as president. He seems to be thinking of the American people and not decisions that waver between two political parties.

What is interesting, is as they talk about separation of church and state, it is conditional. Our money states (Trust in God). We swear (to tell the truth, the whole truth, so help me God) when we take the stand in court.

They have taken God out of the schools, court houses, parks, and anywhere they think it will offend someone. It is sad that our country was founded on the freedom of religion, based by the very first amendment in the constitution, yet politicians strive to use religion as a tool to divide and conquer.

The Democrats are again on the attack trying to dismantle I.C.E. Immigration and Customs Enforcement. I.C.E. was formed on March 1, 2003. They have over 20,000 employees as of 2016. The purpose of I.C.E. is a law enforcement agency of the Federal government of the United States under the jurisdiction of the Department of Homeland Security (DHS). ICE has two primary components: Homeland Security Investigations (HSI) and Enforcement and Removal Operations (ERO). They are Headquartered in Washington, D.C. They are a sister agency of the U.S. Customs and Border Patrol.

Why would any political party wish to dismantle them? It is because the Democrats want open borders. With open borders, comes terrorists, radical Muslims that will infest our towns, cities, states, and country till what we have grown to love and appreciate will exist no more.

President Trump wants to build the wall and secure the borders so that we can still invite others here safely. Common sense has taken over the White House and the Democrats aren't used to it.

ANTI-TRUMP ASSOCIATIONS
ORGANIZATIONS AGAINST AMERICA

Unfortunately, we need to add a chapter on organizations against Trump. It is sad that our president has to be interrupted with organizations that simply want to disrupt his time in office. They want to see him fail as our president. The problem is we elected him to represent us, lead us, and make America great again. These organizations that wish to defy our President, are in fact defying us, the American people.

The following are groups against President Trump. Are these organizations, associations, and clubs the modern day Trojan horse? Are these groups secretly waging war from within for their own agenda?

Our Revolution: On their home page they state the following, "Our Revolution will reclaim democracy for the working people of our country by harnessing the transformative energy of the political revolution." Through supporting a new generation of progressive leaders, empowering millions to fight for progressive change and elevating the political consciousness, Our Revolution will transform American politics to make our political and economic systems once again responsive to the needs of working families."

They talk about a new generation of progressive leaders, meaning favoring or advocating progress, change, improvement, or reform as opposed to wishing to maintain things as they are. This can definitely be good, but bad if it effects changing, altering, or omitting the constitutional rights of Americans.

They mention they want the wealthy and large corporations to pay their share in taxes. They want to stop corporations from shifting their profits and jobs overseas to avoid paying U.S. income taxes. They want to increase the federal minimum wage from $7.25 to $15.00 an hour. Do you think a person that takes your order at a fast-food joint really deserves $15.00 an hour? There are jobs designed at minimum wage for those entering the job market. Jobs like fast-food hamburger joints. If you pay them $15.00 an hour your quick precooked hamburger, just turned in to the same cost as a T-Bone steak. You also have to look at incentive. Some will enjoy working these jobs long term, never giving those out of school a position to fill.

They talked about reversing the trade policies like NAFTA, CAFTA, and PNTR with China. I believe President Trump stated when he ran for president that he was going to bring jobs back to America, or tax corporations that do not comply. He mentioned NAFTA being a bad deal. Why is this organization fighting against Trump? Why are they not working with him? Check out their home page. https://ourrevolution.com/issues/

Sister District Project: On their home page they state the following, "Sister District aims to ensure that all Americans have equal representation and our government works for all people, not just the minority in power. We organize volunteers into local teams based on where they live, and sister this deep blue energy with swing districts across the country to support strategic state races that matter. We are open to volunteers and candidates of all genders. We have a strategic, targeted a focus on critical down-ballot, state races that if we win will make it easier to win national elections." They state deep blue energy, which refers to the Democratic party. They are only focused on winning elections, to control the House and Senate."

They state on their page where they are looking for donations, "Money is the single most important factor that will determine whether a candidate will succeed, especially early in the campaign." They don't tell you anything other than how to give your money to this organization. On one of their other sites they show a united front with many other organizations that have been identified as opposing Trump. https://www.sisterdistrict.com/

Knock Every Door, on their web page they state the following. "It's time we start talking with everybody about the progressive change our country needs. To do this effectively we'll have to take the time to listen to voters who may not agree with us, but could be persuaded to our cause through civil conversations about what matters most in our lives. #KnockEveryDoor is a volunteer-led organization created in the wake of the disastrous 2016 election.

They talked about taking time to listen to those who may disagree with them if they want to be effective. Then they said, but could be persuaded. They have no intention on listening, they want to persuade those they think they can turn their way. The organization was created in the wake of the disastrous 2016 election, according to their web page. This focus is on their party. The welfare of the American people are not their concerns. Their web page is https://knockeverydoor.org/

Swing Left, On their home page they present the slogan It starts with the house. Then they state the following on their homepage, Control of the House in 2018 will be decided by a few Swing Districts, places where the last election was decided by a thin margin. Join your closet Swing District team to hear about things you can do to support Democrats and defeat Republicans in that District no matter where you live. We can stop Trump and the GOP agenda by working together. This is just an obvious organization to support Democrats and resist the Republicans. These organizations do nothing but divide our country.

Flippable, Their web page shows an image of the Senate upside down as they present their slogan, "Our Democracy is upside down." They then state, "With control in a majority of states, the GOP has passed laws to suppress the vote and skew District maps. By electing progressives to state government, we can flip the script and rebuild our democracy. Then they say in the next section, We're supporting 100 candidates to build progressive majorities and restore fair Democracy.

Understand fair Democracy in their eyes is thinking the way they do. They forget to listen to the people that matter, the American people. Their web page is located at https://www.flippable.org/

On their web page they stated "In 2009 With Obama in the White House & Democrats controlling Congress, the GOP was desperate. So they came up with a sneaky, smart solution for winning in the long term: flipping state governments red." This is what we call an election. Flipping states that oppose you, to supporting you? It happens when you have a plan and you explain it to the American people. If they like your plan and how it benefits them, then you will win with their votes.

Resurgent Left: On their web page, they state "Fighting for Team Blue from the bottom up." Every Seat Counts: We support special Democratic candidates in red, blue and purple states, at all levels of government. Our goal is to eliminate all safe seats for Republicans and push the party towards a fifty-state strategy. Flip State Legislatures/Governorships Blue:

We support state-level candidates who can flip state legislatures and governorships blue across the United States, with an eye towards ending the practice of gerrymandering.

I think what they are saying is stop the Republicans gerrymandering, but push for the Blue to continue it, as they try to swing not a few states, but every state Blue. They mention on their page, We connect our candidates with highly reputable and invaluable resources, including campaign managers, tech gurus, media savvy firms, etc. Media Savvy, CNN, MSNBC, and other well known left wing news media networks. Check out their web page at https://www.resurgentleft.org/

What ever happened to check and balance? Why does it have to be either Republican, or Democrat?

Adopt-A-State: Is just another page where the Democratic side wishes to turn the red states blue. It shows a map of the United States and which states are currently Republican, or Democrat.

They mention on their page the following, "Adopting a state is FREE. Adoption is your visual support for Democrats fighting on the conservative front lines. When you adopt a state, it'll post on Facebook and you can tell folks why you adopted them! Once a month we'll send you an email update on the political happenings in your adopted state. We'll also include volunteer opportunities and specific ways to get involved whether it's through the state Democratic Party or one of our Allies." Here they talk about using Face Book as their advertising tool. Face Book has been identified as bias helping Democrats only.

Adopt-A-State web page can be found at,
http://adoptastate.org/

Instead of them focusing on adopting to divide our country, they should adopt to unite us.

Operation 45, on one of their pages they state their mission is the aggressive pursuit of governmental transparency in the service of Democracy. They state in bold letters, "Your donations are critical for us to have the capacity to sue the Trump/Pence administration again and again for documents revealing what is being done with our tax dollars and in our names!"

For them wanting aggressive pursuit of governmental transparency Where is their equal aggressiveness with the Clinton e-mail scandal? They state on their page, Liberating government documents against powerful opposition is what we do. Their definition of liberate is to change Red to Blue. Their web page can be found at, https://wwwgofundme.com/operation-45

They mentioned your donations were for the purpose of suing over and over again. To me this sounds destructive, vengeful, and criminal, such as a hate crime. If at any time I misrepresent an organization here I apologize, but I am using their words and to me this is simply the Democratic Left Wing Party attacking with all cylinders. I think transparency should start with Operation 45. True transparency is being able to see from either side.

I have included the links to these pages so you can view them yourself and make your own unbiased decision.

Movement Voter Project: On their web page they state the following, "What if we could shift 1% of the billions spent on TV adds to local organizing? That's tens of millions for local groups to both win elections and win on issues. MVP is a new way to support directly, the best local groups in key states. Donate to your favorite group, or a featured fund and spread the word.

Are Democrats figuring out that Americans are starting to view the media as an extension of the Liberal Left? Is this why they want to diversify their resources to local areas as they have tainted the media. If you follow the link on their page that says browse all groups you will see 58 other organizations that are all the same. Some are viewed here as we continue. Their web page is located at, https://movement.vote/

The PussyHat Project: On their web page they have a knitted hat. They say, "Put on your hat the fight continues." The Pussyhat Project is a social movement focused on raising awareness about women's issues and advancing human rights by promoting dialogue and innovation through the arts, education and intellectual discourse. The Pussyhat is a symbol of support and solidarity for women's rights and political resistance. Make a hat! Give a hat! Wear your hat! Share a hat!

To me to use the word pussy, lessons the value, it is like calling men's movement DickHeads. Put your condom on and we will fight hard together.

This picture says a lot as we know that Time magazine is anti-Trump. Here we see the PussyHats call themselves the Resistance. That is the bottom line. How long till Time magazine changes its borders from Red to Blue?

They state on their page; We want to establish the PussyHat Network as the information resource hub for all facets of women's rights, a kind of one-stop starting point on the web where people can go to get information about various activities and groups involved across the women's movement. I didn't find any valuable information, other than a spot to donate and throw your money away. Here is their web page link, https://www.pussyhatproject.com/

Latino Victory Project: On their website they mention the following. Building Latino Political Power. "When you don't see people on the ballot that reflect your community, you're less likely to vote. That's why we are making an effort to build Latino political power by investing in Latino Candidates., so that the faces and voices of our community are reflected at every level of government and in the policies that will help drive our country forward.

They state on their website, Latino Victory Foundation is a non-partisan effort to raise awareness about Latinos' contributions to the American society and build greater understanding between Latinos and other communities. The foundation seeks to strengthen the country through conversation and uplift the values of inclusion and civic engagement. Inclusion means to be included in a group or structure.

While I believe it is important to be heard, and that everyone has a right to voice their opinions, including myself. It is also important that we view ourselves first as Americans, above all else. We should not identify ourselves as Republican, Democrat, Hispanic, African American, or any other denomination. Their website is located at http://latinovictory.us/our-work/

Emerge America: On their website they state, "We inspire women to run, we hone their skills to win." They comment under announcements, more women involved in Democratic politics. It's our time: meet 18 candidates leading the historic rise of Black women running for office in Alabama. They have a link on Face Book where they mention its pride month and we're celebrating all the LGBTQIA women in politics who are blazing trails and breaking down barriers. They mention on their webpage, Gender politics in America has come front and center since Hillary Clinton lost the 2016 presidential election and the Me Too movement. Here they talk about the women movement, then Black women movement, and then the LGBTQIA movement. This is nothing but covering your bases as you try to unite all women no matter your standards, or beliefs.

Do they view Hillary Clinton as a great leader or as a liar, and part of the Me movement? They mentioned her on their webpage, so either they like her attributes, or dislike them.

Emily's List: Is located in Washington D.C. It is an organization for pro-choice Democratic women. On their page they state, "We ignite change by getting pro-choice Democratic women elected to office. It is strictly a page to donate your money. It gives you a cause, but that is all. When their sole purpose is to collect money, while giving very little information on their accomplishments, makes me wonder.

Indivisible: On their webpage they come out swinging as they mention, "We must stop Brett Kavanaugh from becoming Trump's next Supreme Court Justice." They also state, "Our mission is to fuel a progressive grassroots network of local groups to resist the Trump Agenda. In every congressional district in the country, people like you are starting local groups and leading local actions. Are you standing indivisible with us? Then sign up for weekly actions and updates. They mention, we are not the leaders of this movement you are. Why send updates if you are not the leader? They should be receiving them, not sending them.

This is not correct, They are the leaders as they purposely direct others on what their agenda should be. What about the Americans who support trump? Why are their voices not being heard? It comes down to the Democratic party attacking Trump and the American people. They want resistance with the Supreme Court nominee. They are leading this fight.

Run for Something: On their webpage they state the following. "Much to our surprise and absolute delight, Run for Something is more than just a side project or pop-up organization for a single election cycle it's a movement of millennials ready to run, lead, and change the world.

We've seen "run for something!!" become a mantra for those fed up with Trump, frustrated with the status quo, and eager to take action in their communities by becoming the decision-makers themselves. We've been overjoyed as our Twitter followers became our candidates who then became elected officials.

We've certainly felt both smug and gratified as our "run everywhere" operating theory that was once considered odd, has become conventional wisdom and throughout it all, we've learned about how to grow, experiment, fail, and try again. This they were taught by the Trump organization as President Trump used Twitter like never before.

I know that President Trump was labeled as ridiculous and a mad Tweeter as he has used it to keep the media in check, as they tried purposely distorting the truth, facts, or anything that helped the Republican party, while hurting the Democratic party. Now the Democratic side that states on this webpage that what seemed odd has become conventional wisdom. These webpages, along with other media conglomerates, like Face Book, Twitter, You Tube, and more are the very tools the Democrats are using to promote the Democratic Progressive Movement Check out their webpage, https://runforsomething.net/

Wellstone: On their webpage they state the following. "Founded to carry forward the work of Paul and Sheila Wellstone, we arm progressives with the strategies and skills to win. We develop political leaders. We strengthen movement organizations. We ignite change." These are all familiar sayings as though they are all designed by a particular group, or groups that encompass the Democratic party. On their map they are targeting 5 different states, Minnesota, Colorado, Texas, Florida, and Maryland. They state on the page, "We're up against conservatives who will stop at nothing to weaken our power, and create an America where everyone's on their own."

This should make us sad, as they say things to inflame progressives into believing, Republicans are just about themselves. At what point does the word conservative turn bad? At what point will Democrats return to the tables to negotiate as Americans and not as Democrats? This goes for those Republicans as well. President Trump is trying to unite us, but as you see there are many organizations blowing smoke to cloud the issues, for their own agendas.

The web pages on some of these sites do seem very similar in many ways. Maybe they are all using one of those build your own website places. We have covered approximately 15 organizations so far. As we continue on, think about what their agenda is. So far they seem only to focus on donation, persuading others to join their cause, and to resist the President and the American people. Their site is located at, https://www.wellstone.org/impact

She Should Run: This page starts off with 250,000 by 2030. They state join us to get 250,000 women running for elected office by 2030. They state "Join She Should Run and expand the talent pool of women running for office. Are they searching for talented people who are female, or are they searching for women to fill positions that will politically adapt to their surroundings?

They have an image of two barbie dolls on their webpage, which to me reflects a fantasy world, much like getting that many women in to fill those positions. How many positions are there available between now and 2030? They talk about expanding the talent pool, or do they just mean filling it with female bodies?

I have no problem voting for a woman, but I am going to go off her experience, her agenda that she presents, and her character. I will judge her according to her merits. And not her sex, or race. If the roles were reversed, they would call this sexism as they would be stating We want 250,000 more men to join the political arena. I think it should be about quality, not quantity. 250,000 seems extreme to me.

Once again they try separating political seats here by women and had brought up that 90 Muslims have ran this election cycle. The most since September 11, 2001. Not sure how we should interpret that. Why can't we work together, rather than opposing one another? These organizations focus on empowering one group while putting another down. It may not be intentional, it may not be obvious, but the end result is striving for 250,000 women by 2030.

This is another example of reverse discrimination. Their website can be found at http://www.sheshouldrun.org/

Higher Heights: This webpage promotes Black women for political offices. I think that is great, but then on their page they state Sista to watch, which means proud Black women who carries herself with pride. This is confusing as they don't want to be discriminated as Black women, yet they use words that separate Blacks from others. They also mention on one of their pages, 2018 Grammy Awards. Is this page sponsored by actors? They mentioned that only a handful of Black female artists have been nominated for awards despite the overwhelming influence Black women have on the music industry. They also mentioned We know women of color in Congress and every level of public office can relate. Despite making up one of the most consistent voting demographics in the nation, we are still woefully under-represented in public office.

When they state themselves as under-represented are they looking at the total number of Americans, or are they trying to say they should have equal what the Caucasians do, even though Caucasians outnumber the Blacks by millions.

Their webpage states, "Higher Heights is building a national strategy to mobilize one million Black women and dollars by 2020 in order to harness their collective economic and voting power." These organizations have only one agenda, divide and conquer.

President Obama divided our nation with racism, poverty, religion, while promoting Muslim-hood, shaming Christians and our patriotic soldiers, and those that flew the American flag with pride. Many times he spoke without the American flag present. To me this is un-American.

American Civil Liberties Union: On their web page they mention the following, "The family separation crisis is the direct result of the Trump administration policy choices, driven by the view that immigrants and asylum seekers deserve nothing but cruelty and punishment.

They also stated, "We are in the courts, streets, and in Congress to hold the Trump administration accountable for the irreparable damage it has done to these young lives. We need you in this fight."

I think first we need to ask the right questions and attach blame to the appropriate people. While they wish to label Trump's organization, which is the American people, as cruel. What do you call illegal immigrants that put their own children's health and welfare at risk? These organizations would cry if you left your kid in a car alone when it is 90 degrees outside, yet they say nothing of these children walking alone unattended without their parents in the desert.

They have no food or water, where criminals patrol frequently preying on the weak. They know their children are at risk, but choose to put their needs ahead of their children as their plan is to come in after, as they beg to be reunited with the very children they sent over separating themselves from.

I call this neglect, abandonment, and cruel. If they kept their children with them, they would not have to go through the punishment of separation which they chose to do.

If the ACLU is serious about this, they will hold those illegal immigrants accountable for their actions.

Anti-Defamation League: On their page You will find these statements. "The vacancy left by Justice Kennedy's retirement is a critical one for the future of civil rights, civil liberties, and our democracy. At a time where hard-fought progress in LGBT rights, voting rights, and women's rights are threatened, and immigrants and vulnerable communities in our country are under attack, the role of an independent Supreme Court and one that protects the Constitutional rights of all Americans is more important than ever.

"The entire world held its breath as 12 Thai young boys were trapped. Yet here in this country thousands of children have been separated from their parents and trapped behind bars." Fred Lawrence

Let us get real here, these organizations that wish to compare 12 young boys that were guided by an appropriate adult to illegal immigrants that were abandoned by their parents for the purpose of manipulating the system to get their foot in the door, or on U.S. soil is ridiculous. These children they talk about that are trapped are safe from criminal elements, sheltered, and fed. To say they are suffering inhumanely is wrong.

Comparing the two together shows the idiocy of those that speak on this subject Their slogan is "Imagine a world without hate." So why do they push hate through passive channels? Why do they defy our President, the American people, and those that are not Democrats?

They call themselves Anti-Defamation League, but they are all about damaging the Republicans and President Trump, who we elected.

Black Lives Matter: Is an organization that has been under a lot of scrutiny. Their website is located at the following site. http://www.blacklifematters.org/

On their page they mention, We stand against all forms of police brutality, excessive force and profiling. Here is a list of young people who have lost their lives due to all the above.

John Crawford, Ezell Ford, Dante Parker, Eric Garner, Darius Simmons, Chavis Carter, James Brissette, Malissa Williams, Timothy Russell, Victor Steen, Ramarely Graham, Noel Polanco, Reginald Doucet, Ervin Jefferson, Steven Eugene, Ousmane Zongo, Aaron Campbell, Sean Bell, Wendell Allen, Oscar Grant, Alonzo Ashley, Amadou Diallo, Timothy Stansbury, Jordan Davis, Orlando Barlow, Tony Francis, Danroy Henry, Darrin Hanna, Ronald Madison, Nathaniel Jones, Rekia Boyd, Kendric McDade, Trayvon Martin.

If we look at **Trayvon Martin,** you will notice they use a picture of him when he was young making him look like an innocent child. Trayvon was a young man tattooed up and was 6 foot 2 inches and 175 lbs.

He also was not killed by the cops he was killed by a Hispanic man by the name George Zimmerman.

Kendric McDade was 19 years old and was portrayed as a loving person in the picture presented on their webpage holding a baby.

He was killed as he fled from the police who were responding to an armed robbery report. Kendric then turned heading towards a cruiser with his hand near his waist.

The officer feared for his life and shot Kendric after he failed to comply with the officers instructions.

Rekia Boyd was shot while in a crowd by an off-duty police officer. The officer had gotten in a verbal altercation and the officer supposedly seen the other person pull what he thought was a gun from his waistband. He shot his gun fearing for his life and she was struck and killed. The officer was found not guilty.

Nathaniel Jones, Was not killed by police, Jerron Washington of Milwaukee who was sentenced to ten years in prison and eight years extended supervision in connection with the shooting death of Nathaniel Jones on Monday, June 23rd. A judge also order Washington to pay $2,500 in restitution.

Ronald Madison, and **James Brissette** were both gunned down, and the officers involved were finally brought to justice.

This happened when two groups of families and friends, all of them black, were crossing the Danziger bridge in search of food and relatives when police officers rushed to the scene in a Budget rental truck. The officers, responding to a distress call, opened fire with shotguns and AK-47s, sending those on the bridge, all of whom were unarmed, diving and running for cover. This was back during Hurricane Katrina.

Darrin Hanna The Lake County State's Attorney's Office in March 2012 declined to charge any of the officers involved, saying they used a "reasonable force" after responding to a domestic incident.

Hanna told responding officers to shoot him and then fought with them before he was subdued, prosecutors said. He died in a hospital a week after the confrontation.

Danroy Henry, 20, of Easton, a junior at Pace University in New York, was shot and killed by police outside a bar in Pleasantville, N.Y. early on Sunday, Oct. 17, 2010. His friend and fellow Oliver Ames High School graduate Brandon Cox and another young man were in the car with him. Some of these cases are legit as officers are caught in lies, or evidence that points in another direction. These are a few names they presented. Some of these cases, try presenting the victim as innocent, rather than the perpetrator.

Here they want every Black victim to be seen as innocent when in fact we no better. Some may be while others are not.

The BLM is focused on spreading, directing, and justifying hate, rather than searching for fair, impartial justice, by following the facts and using the courts to make an argument. Many of these members wish to protest, rally, and encourage others to fall into the mob like mentality.

The BLM only focus on promoting Black lives rather than American Lives. They say end ignorance, but ignorance is being directed by them as they yell pigs in a blanket, rob, loot, steal, and destroy.

They have the word unite on their webpage yet scream to be separated, excluded, and heard throughout the local and national communities. They say all lives matter, do they?

Border Angels On their web page they say Border Angels helps to save lives of immigrants. They say, "Border Angels prevents unnecessary deaths and harm reduction through desert water drops, border rescue stations and day laborer outreach."

Is it possible their helping, actually enables? It creates an avenue for illegals to follow knowing where supplies will be located at as they journey illegally on.

They state on their page, "Border Angels provides alternative break and education programs including: Internships and community awareness of issues surrounding undocumented migrants, immigrations and border issues."

Does this educational information assist them in learning better ways to enter and stay here as illegals? Do they educate them on the actual procedures of how to enter our country legally?

They mention thousands of refugees from earthquake stricken Haiti are stuck in Tijuana, while they ask for refugee support in Baja, California. They mention on their webpage education not deportation.

This organization is definitely not supporting the President of the United States, or the welfare of our country.

There is a reason that President Trump got elected. There is a reason for building the wall and securing our borders. I say Go American, or Go Home.

Center for Reproductive Rights On their webpage it starts right off with, "Judge Kavanaugh's nomination, we may face the greatest risk to the future of the reproductive rights in the United States. Join the fight to defend the constitutional right to abortion.

This organization is really trying to prevent a judge that has done a good, if not a great job from getting in as a Supreme Court Justice, strictly because they fear what he might do rather than what he has done. The Democrats have made it clear that they want to pick the next Supreme Court Justice, one that will favor their views. On their page in their words they say, it could shift the balance of the Supreme Court.

If you are Pro-life, you will be seen as the bad guy. As we look at all these groups, we see lots of diversity. Some believe, all life should be saved. Others feel it is a woman's right to abort, and the government should not get involved. I see both sides to this and while I support both sides equally, I would have to review each circumstance individually, the same as with the death sentence. I would not manipulate the Supreme Court Justice by trying to sway it one way or the other.

As we identify these other groups on here, do not judge them without first checking out their webpages. Review them as we have all of these and be your own judge.

Remember, I am identified as a Deplorable, so I may be bias. Look at the names of these organizations. The names say a lot.

Groups against the Trump organization.

Coalition for Humane Immigrant Rights of LA

Council on America Islamic Relations

Equality California

Esperanza Immigrant Rights Project

Heal the Bay

 Los Angeles Boys and Girls Club

Los Angeles LGBT Center

NAACP Los Angeles

Planned Parenthood Los Angeles

Rainn

Running Start

We the Protesters

There were three groups I checked out that are identified as anti-Trump, but their pages appeared at least legit. They were Ignite, Big Brothers Big Sisters of Greater Los Angeles, and California Women's Law Center.

There are more groups, but this gives you an idea of the type of resistance he is having to deal with.

When I went to check out the Republican parties that were against the Democrats, I was directed right back to Democrats against the Trump organizations. I did not find any Republican organization that targeted specifically the Democrats. I am not saying there are none out there, but the Democrats have flooded the internet like a virus seeking to disrupt, resist, and stall on any progress President Trump attempts to accomplish.

If I started a webpage, it might look like this.

https://GOD BLESS AMERICA

Together we can rebuild our country with stronger borders. We can build our economy by bringing jobs back to America and lowering taxes for the middle class. We can stop labeling crime as racism and start holding criminals accountable. We can start taking pride in our men in blue. We can take care of our military veterans, and give them the tools, weapons, and emotional support they need.

We can talk about God without fear of persecution. Democrats and Republicans will once again unite. We will become American Strong, and American Reliable.

Racism will someday be gone as we all work together building America with Americans.

President Trump has signed over 63 Executive Orders, which we have covered earlier. He has shown us that he is not a president that talks, but one of action as he continues to gets results.

He seems to always be one step ahead of the media, the Democrats, and those hate groups, that wish to speak on the behalf of a select few, through violence. He is about honoring and securing our constitutional rights. He is not focused on being politically correct, but rather morally correct.

North Korea has started dismantling some of there nuclear sites. They have started returning some of our dead American soldiers back to U.S. soil.

Russian leader Vladimir Putin and President Trump are attempting to build better relations with each other. Why can't our Democrats and Republicans work on building better relationship with one another?

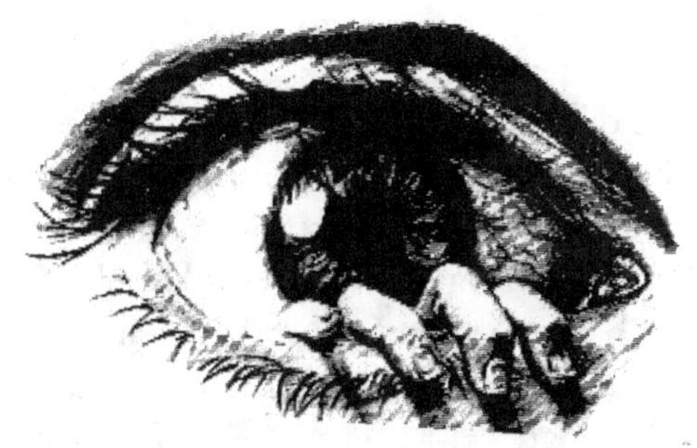

THE FINAL THOUGHTS
UNITING AMERICANS

Let us remember where we once were. We were once with a president that refused to show his birth certificate to verify his legitimacy. Barack Obama, is a politician who served as the 44th President of the United States from January 20, 2009 till January 20, 2017. During his time in office he created the Obama Care, which left Americans with bad medical coverage.

He incited riots within his own borders and caused a great divide, as he identified Blacks killed, not as criminals that resisted or would not comply, but as victims. He supported the rioting, looting, and total chaos, by justifying the racial riots were due to bad, corrupt, and racist police.

He appeared to ignore the facts on gun control as he kept saying we need stricter gun laws, yet in the city of Chicago they have some of the strictest gun regulations, laws, and policies. Yet, Chicago has become a war zone.

He changed how other countries looked at us by his actions. Through him we were seen as weak and vulnerable.

He bowed to the king of Saudi Arabia rather than stand as the President of the United States and shake his hand. He negotiated with terrorists releasing 5 Taliban from Guantanamo Bay. They were Abdel Ghaib Ahmad Hakim, Salah Mohammed Salih Al-Dhabi, Abdul Khaled Al-Baydani, Hashim Bin Ali Bin Amor Sliti, and Husayn Salim Muhammad Al-Mutari Yafai. He shouted from the White House, on how proud we should be of Bergdahl, a traitor to our country.

President Obama talked in shame of Christians as he supported the Muslim community first before the lives of Americans. He supported Reverend Wright who preached not the word of God, but the word of hate as he was racist against the White community. He often spoke out both sides of his mouth as he said, he was against same-sex marriages, then the next time said he supported them.

The last thing I wanted to bring up on him is that he served 8 years as the President of the United States, but if you watched him on television as he spoke to the American people, our flag started showing up less and less behind him and other symbols were then placed behind him.

My personal opinion is he was never for America. All we have to do is look at Obama.org.

This is our former President of the United States Obama's website below, check it out.

Will he become King Obama?

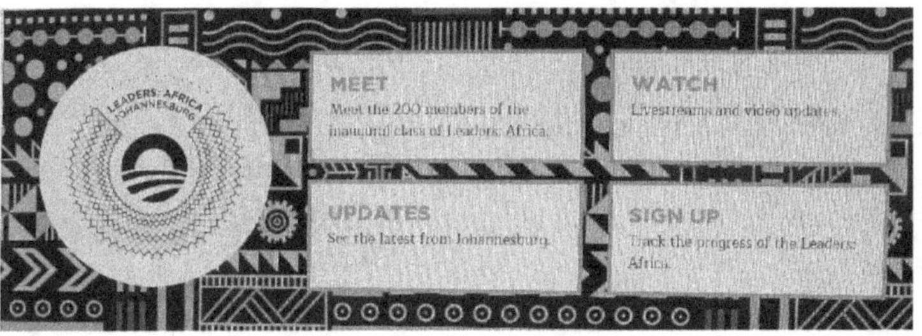

Do any of these symbols, or patterns look familiar as backdrop when he spoke as president?

Does he have any page out there trying to help Americans?, homeless, our military veterans, or just those from Africa?

President Obama with the aid of Hillary Clinton helped create our newest president Donald Trump, for that we should thank them. They united the middle class and those in the Christian communities to come together and become identified as Deplorable people in a basket.

President Obama stood by and did nothing when police were assassinated, when football players took a knee, and when our flag was burned in protests across America.

The great depression is over we have a new president, President Donald Trump who will lead us with commonsense, pride, and America first attitude.

We should not forget the things that built our country in the first place. I remember going to school, and the first thing we would do was say the Pledge of Allegiance.

The Pledge of Allegiance

I pledge allegiance to the flag of the United States of America and to the Republic for which it stands, one nation under God, indivisible, with liberty and justice for all.

This was a part of our history, and through time those that wanted to disrupt our nation by arguing on the word God in the pledge of allegiance have pried this historic document out of our American children's hands.

The Star Spangled Banner

The Star Spangled Banner by Francis Scott Key 1814. This has become our National Anthem.

Oh can you see, by the dawns early light, what so proudly we hailed at the twilight's last gleaming, whose broad stripes and bright stars thru the perilous fight, o'er the ramparts we watched were so gallantly streaming and the rocket's red glare, the bombs bursting in air, gave proof through the night that our flag was still there. Oh, say does that star spangled banner yet wave. O'er the land of the free and the home of the brave.

The story that goes with that song has deep emotional value as American after American went to hold our flag up in a battle, never surrendering our flag that could have changed our history books.

Those NFL players that make hundred of thousands of dollars and choose to take a knee during the national anthem are not only disrespecting our country, our soldiers and countrymen who fought for our freedom. They show themselves as rude and ignorant, not waiting for the proper time. They view themselves as entitled due to their color.

The colors that matter should be our flag's colors. Red, White, and Blue. Those that protest using our flag in a disrespectful manner are the ones crying to be protected under the same flag they disrespect.

President Donald Trump has told us what he was going to attempt while in office. He has so far been doing just that. He has accomplished more in his short stay then President Obama did in his 8 years. Our economy is up, along with morale. Unemployment is down. The Racism is deescalating, police are not being viewed and targeted as they were under the Obama administration. Isis is being dealt with and are being eliminated like never before. President Trump's Executive orders actually make sense, putting America first. This is not about Republican vs. Democrat, it is about Americans uniting as one. It is uniting to better America. No president has, is, or will be perfect. We need to remember we are all human. Each chapter covers areas of controversy, but nothing we can't overcome together as Americans. I do not judge by color, only actions. Color yourself with pride, respect, politeness, honor, and most of all love.

I titled this book America's Deplorables, not to just mock Hillary Clinton, but to make a stand.

Americans want to be heard, we want fair representation on both sides without being insulted, demoralized as deplorable people in a basket. This book is about uniting Americans together. I did not vote for a party for president. I voted for a president that had character, charisma, and most of all integrity. I voted for a president that would try to live up to his word, and not say what he thought we wanted to hear. He is not perfect, no one is.

I voted for Donald Trump because, he is not politically correct. He said what I felt. He touched true Americans like never before. I look forward to his second term in office. I believe in the end he will unite both the Democratic and Republican parties.

We should be fair and look at the Democratic party a second. What are their goals? Do they want secure borders? Do they want to lower taxes? Are they wanting to protect your second amendment right? Do they want to increase the job market, or hourly wage?

These are just some of the questions that divide the parties. I know I can tell you their number one goal is to resist President Trump who is making them look stupid, guilty, and corrupt. They know that while he succeeds in office, he is showing the American people what the Democrats couldn't, or wouldn't do in the last eight years.

He is draining the Washington swamps, one politician at a time.

I wrote this book because I was fed up with the bureaucracy that lingered in Washington D.C.. President Trump came in an outsider and was attacked by both parties, as they tried laughing at him, belittling him like he wasn't worthy to be in their presence. I believed in him from the beginning as I wrote the book Changing America 2016. It covered everything we have been addressing in this book.

Americans agree that political correctness has its place in politics, but not at the cost of the American people. It is time for Washington D.C. to clean house and hold each other accountable for their actions. President Trump is not afraid to say he is an American, he is male, and he is White. This is who he is. He is also a president that has donated his presidential paycheck to worthy organizations, such as the Veterans and Educational departments.

Donald Trump became president because myself and millions more believe in him. He has made a difference already. There are more changes coming. They will produce positive results for Americans. This book is just the beginning of his term. President Trump will not be truly appreciated till many years later, but for the Deplorable ones, we know and appreciate all he is doing today.

Let's Make America Great Again.

The **Changing America series** was created after one American saw his country being desecrated by not just

the blacks, but the Democratic party, including then President Obama. He had an opportunity to qualm his country, but rather fueled it with fire as he justified racial riots as understandable. He refused to identify Muslim extremist for who they were. He ignored our flag as it screamed for justice and protection from radical protestors.

Changing America Volume II was a continuance of the first book as our country was being torn apart and challenged with political correctness. This book showed our country falling right before our eyes. The Obama regime was dismantling our country, economically, militarily, and morally.

Changing America 2016 is like the knight in shinning armor. It was time for a new Commander in Chief. One that could lead with confidence and pride. Donald Trump stood up and stepped forward, as he volunteered his services to be our next President.

He was challenged by all, Republicans, Democrats, News media, and of course the out of touch celebrities. I knew he would win, because he said everything we needed to hear, and not what we wanted to hear. He focused on Border security, immigration, crime, and protecting our constitutional rights.

America's Deplorables have united like the minute men of the past. We have come together in force to save our country. President Trump is leading the way as we take back our country that the Liberals were giving away.

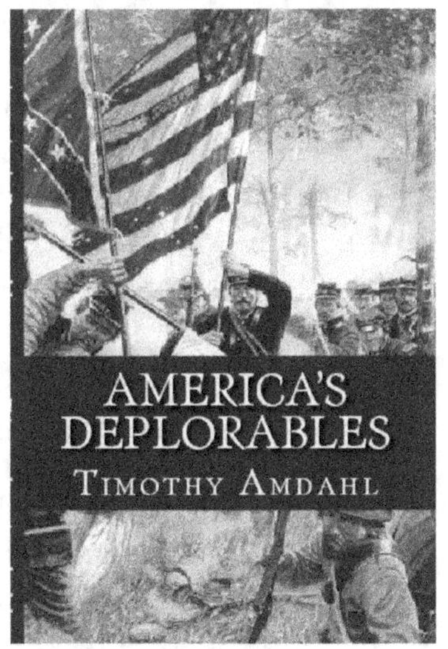

Making America Great Again

ABOUT THE AUTHOR

Tim Amdahl is a 1981 High School graduate of Estherville Iowa. He was raised in a small town where family values and bonds were strong. He served two years in the army, then transferred to the Marines serving four years with them. He was assigned to protect the Commander of the Sixth Fleet, Admiral Martin who was an eight year P.O.W. and Admiral Kelso who took over as Commander Sixth Fleet Strike Force South Southern Europe. He served as a youth counselor for multiple agencies, working in positive peer cultures, behavior modification programs, and sexual predator units. He has served in security as a security guard at a Nuclear Power Plant; He is currently working for the Illinois Department of Corrections as a Correctional Officer, with over eighteen years' experience. He had volunteered his services working for the sheriff Department at different times. He has written many books on politics, conspiracies, and technologies.

Tim Amdahl is just your average American who has served his country and works 40 hours a week. He is raising his family trying to be a positive, productive citizen in his community. He loves God, his country, and family and friends. GOD BLESS AMERICA.